A Heart

Broken Open

A Heart Broken Open

Radical faith in an age of fear

RAY GASTON

First published 2009 by
Wild Goose Publications, 4th Floor, Savoy House, 140 Sauchiehall St,
Glasgow G2 3DH, UK.
Wild Goose Publications is the publishing division
of the Iona Community.
Scottish Charity No. SCO03794.
Limited Company Reg. No. SCO96243.

www.ionabooks.com

ISBN 978-1-905010-61-5

The publishers gratefully acknowledge the support of the Drummond
Trust, 3 Pitt Terrace, Stirling FK8 2EY in producing this book.

A catalogue record for this book is available from the British Library.

Overseas distribution:
Australia: Willow Connection Pty Ltd, Unit 4A, 3-9 Kenneth Road,
Manly Vale, NSW 2093
New Zealand: Pleroma, Higginson Street, Otane 4170,
Central Hawkes Bay
Canada: Novalis/Bayard Publishing & Distribution,
10 Lower Spadina Ave., Suite 400, Toronto, Ontario M5V 2Z2

Printed by Lightning Source

Contents

Acknowledgements

This book has had a very long gestation period! Many of the chapters started their life in another form. Chapters two and three were developed out of a presentation of story and song that Julie Greenan and I put together for the Together for Peace festival in Leeds in 2003, called 'Resistance and Love – Spirituality for Non-violent Struggle' and performed at St Anne's Cathedral, Leeds with later versions being performed at Northern Friends Peace Board in 2004 and at the Peace School in August 2007. Chapter four was developed through dialogue at various events organised within the Shi'a community in England and Iraq. During my time in Iraq I was invited to address a conference at Karbala University on a Christian's view of the relevance of Imam Hussein to the current situation in Iraq, which I entitled 'Is This Liberation?'. I was also invited to reflect on my experience in Iraq with the Shi'a community in England at events organised by the Ahlul Bayt Islamic Centre, Leeds, the Baab-Ul-Ilm in Shadwell, Leeds, the Behlool Society at the Masjid-Al-Husayn in Leicester and the Al Mahdi Institute in Birmingham. I am grateful for the quality of discussion and dialogue at all these events which helped me shape the final versions of the chapters of this book. Chapter six began life as a sermon delivered at All Hallows Church during Ramadan 2005,[1] entitled 'Lamentation and Love: "Natural" Disasters and Worship of the Triune God', a version of which appeared in the journal *Contact: Practical Theology and Pastoral Care (Vol. 153),* in 2006; this final version was delivered as a sermon in the chapel at the Queen's Foundation for Ecumenical Theological Education, in Ramadan 2009.

I am grateful to Annie, Firdaws and Hussein for their generous and thoughtful contributions to the Dialogue section of this book and to Salma for her powerful and considered introduction. Thanks also go to Neil Paynter at Wild Goose for his tireless work on getting my manuscript up to scratch for publication.

I would also like to thank folk at the Makkah Masjid and the Grand Mosque in Hyde Park, Leeds who were always so welcoming and friendly to the rather strange Christian priest who often turned up to *jummah* prayers on a Friday. Hyde Park is blessed with two wonderful mosques that are increasingly engaged with their local communities and interfaith issues in Leeds and seeking to challenge Islamophobia with hospitality and openness.

I am grateful to the Bishop of Ripon and Leeds, John Packer, for his unstinting support throughout my ministry at All Hallows, and to Peter Burrows, the Archdeacon of Leeds, for his active encouragement and help from 2005 onwards, and particularly for arranging a summer sabbatical in 2007 that enabled me to complete the first draft of this book. I am indebted to my friend Sheena McMain for providing me with a bolt-hole in which to complete the first draft of the book during that summer.

Finally, I would like to thank the congregation at All Hallows and the folk of Hyde Park, Leeds for the privilege of ministering with and amongst them for eight years between 1999 and 2007. This book is about only a very small part of that ministry. All Hallows is a unique and vibrant Christian community with a wonderfully broad and inclusive vision and ministry – check it out if you are ever in the vicinity of Leeds!

I dedicate this book to Peter Dale, Christian pacifist and

friend to people of other faiths, whose quiet and persistent witness to peace and interfaith dialogue for many years is an inspiration to me.

I also offer this book in memory of two friends, both mentioned in these pages, who influenced and challenged me during my time in Hyde Park. Professor Hafiz Fateh Muhammad, Imam and scholar, and Pat Regan, mother, community activist and woman of faith. May they rest in peace and rise in glory.

Ray Gaston

Footnote

1. I have used the year of the Gregorian calendar throughout the book, even when referring to Islamic months, for reasons of brevity. The Islamic calendar of course is different, not only in its lunar nature – being 11 days shorter than the Gregorian calendar – but also because the first year of the Islamic calendar is dated from the time Muhammad and his followers emigrated to Yathrib, later known as Medina, from Mecca. This event, known as the Hijrah, happened in 622 of the Common Era – which would mean Ramadan 2005 CE was 1426 AH.

Introduction

Salma Yaqoob

The spiritual journey in this book spoke to me in a very personal way. Ray Gaston's story about the redemptive power of solidarity reflects my own experience. In the immediate aftermath of the terrible events of 9/11, I – like all other Muslims I knew – felt the most crushing sense of isolation. All of us knew our world as we had hitherto experienced it was about to be changed for ever. We worried about what the future held. Some of us experienced physical and verbal abuse. We gathered in each other's homes and debated about what countries we could emigrate to if things really got bad. The impact on me of any solidarity was profound. My experience of it came from non-believers, socialists and atheists who were inspired into action by their own sense of morality. It was also provided by Christians who opened their church doors for the anti-war movement to meet when many mosques were nervous to do so.

The experience of engagement in a mass anti-war movement, of marching side by side with tens of thousands of others, the majority non-Muslim, united in their solidarity with the people of Afghanistan and Iraq with whom they shared neither faith nor culture but a sense of humanity, did more to enhance a sense of Britishness in myself and other Muslims than any number of government citizenship classes! The story Ray tells of the solidarity his congregation provided to their Muslim neighbours is a profound and uplifting one. It was actions like these that helped me through the dark and difficult times, that gave me hope.

Ray hopes his book will serve to encourage in some small

way a greater dialogue and understanding between Muslims and Christians. He already has had that effect on me, through both his moving account of the practical ways he has reached out to Muslims (and his moral courage in being prepared to pay a price for doing so) and his frank reflections on his personal spiritual journey. These reflections were at once recognisable in that many of the issues he has grappled with, e.g. in terms of sincerity of intention, viewing political action for social justice through the prism of spirituality, examination of the practical implications of standing by moral principles, are ones that I have grappled with as a Muslim. They are particularly fascinating, however, in giving an insight into a Christian-specific framework. Furthermore, Ray shares how he examined his own beliefs through his interactions with Muslims, and was able to combine elements of Islamic thought and practice in a way that strengthened his own Christian faith and practice. By acting as an agent of change and at the same time being open to change himself, Ray exemplifies a powerful alternative to the polarising discourse which views difference as a threat, and entrenches people's positions with no potential for enrichment or development.

His book emphasises the need for dialogue between people of faith on the essence of what it means to love God. It is also very much a call to people of all faiths to examine how they relate their faith to action in the here and now, especially in relation to the poor and marginalised. The message of the gospels speaks to us today, and through them the message of Jesus is one that many Muslims, who also claim to love Jesus, would benefit from being reminded of:

'I was hungry and you gave me food; I was thirsty and you gave me drink; I was a stranger and you welcomed me; I was

naked and you clothed me; I was sick and you visited me; I was in prison and you came to me.' And when the righteous answered that they didn't recall doing any of these things, he said, 'As you did it to one of the least of these my brethren, you did it to me.'

In this post-9/11 world, intolerance and racism are increasing. In most Western countries their primary driver is Islamophobia, but intolerance against one minority group feeds intolerance against all. In Switzerland, a referendum is to be held on banning minarets throughout the country.[1] In Germany, France and Scandinavia debate rages over the right of Muslim women to wear Islamic dress. During the American Presidential campaign Republican and Democratic candidates were busy visiting Christian and Jewish groups, while keeping a safe distance from the large Muslim community. As one commentator notes: 'In electoral terms, American Muslims are the new untouchables.'[2]

The insidious, morally corrupting nature of racism was captured in the photographs of Italian holidaymakers on a beach outside Naples, continuing to sunbathe close to the bodies of two drowned Roma sisters, apparently indifferent to their deaths.[3] Ugly voices from the past are gaining confidence. The new 'post-fascist' mayor of Rome was welcomed in the heart of the city by hundreds of supporters who greeted him with straight-armed fascist salutes and chants of 'Duce! Duce!' Emboldened by a growing climate of intolerance, the Italian government has authorised the fingerprinting of the entire Roma population. Jewish community leaders warn that the measure could eventually lead to 'exclusion from schools, separated classes and widespread discrimination'. Alarmed at the growing climate of racism, Pope Benedict has reminded Catholics that it is their duty to steer others in society away from 'racism, intolerance and exclusion [of others]'.[4] An editorial in Italy's most popular Catholic weekly, *Famiglia Cristiana,* speculated as to whether fascism was returning to Italy under another guise.[5]

In a poll on Islamophobia for the *Dispatches* programme, a third of Britain's Muslims said they or their family members have suffered abuse or hostility since 7/7, and over two-thirds of the wider British public thought that prejudice against Muslims has increased. Yet, at the same time, a majority of the public also continues to believe that the religion of Islam is to blame for the bombings.[6] The association of Islam and all Muslims with a sinister and dangerous faith runs deep, and the hostility and suspicion with which Muslims are now viewed is something we are very much aware of. I worry about the kind of society my young children will come to adulthood in.

What responsibility do people of faith have in a world marked by intolerance and injustice? Surely, it must be to bear witness. To not allow ourselves to become indifferent to all God's children. To not allow our hearts to harden. To recognise the humanity of others and in the process reaffirm our own. All believers are united in our love and devotion to God. Our redemption and salvation lies in our realisation of that love. And what more profound realisation than our conscious efforts to awaken God's love in all those around us. For me the process in which the individual strives for his or her highest potential cannot be separated from the broader socio-political context in which we live. The more we are indifferent to injustice, poverty, war and oppression, the more spiritually diminished we become. The more we struggle against such injustices, the more we continuously widen the doors of our hearts to others, the more enriched spiritually we become, the closer we are to God. This is a dialectical interaction between the struggle to raise our inner spirituality and our engagement with our external world. The writer and political activist Arundhati Roy provides a hymn of conscious reflection on both, which speaks to me as profoundly as many a prayer: '*To love. To be loved. To never forget your own insignificance. To never get used to the unspeakable violence and the vulgar disparity of life around you. To seek joy in the saddest places. To pursue beauty to its lair. To never simplify what is complicated or complicate what is simple. To respect strength, never power. Above all, to watch. To try and understand. To never look away. And never, never, to forget.*'

To bear witness. To seek the connection between our internal and external worlds. To love in the name of God.

Salma Yaqoob, 2008

Footnotes

1. 'This Persecution of Gypsies Is Now the Shame of Europe', Seumas Milne, *The Guardian*, Thursday, July 10, 2008

2. 'The New Untouchables', Lawrence Swaim, www.infocusnews.net/content/view/24264/615/

3. 'Italy's Gypsies Suffer Discrimination and Prospect of Draconian Curbs', *The Guardian*, Monday, July 21, 2008

4. 'Pope Appears to Back Warning about Fascism', John Hooper, *The Guardian*, Tuesday, August 19, 2008

5. 'Rise of the Right', Martin Jacques, www.guardian.co.uk, Wednesday, April 30, 2008

6. *Dispatches* is a Channel 4 news, politics and current events programme, www.channel4.com

Solidarity

Chapter one

Challenging Islamophobia

My friend runs a successful café in Hyde Park in Leeds, frequented by a very mixed clientele and popular with students in term times. His business by all accounts appears to be booming, but he talks of selling up and moving, not out of Leeds, but out of the UK. He is a Muslim, brought up in this country by parents who to all intents fitted the model of the media and government's 'integrated Muslim'. His father, who came over to the UK from Kashmir, fought for the British Army. A picture of the Queen adorned their living room alongside verses from the Qur'an and a picture of Mecca. A decade ago my friend would even have been seen drinking the odd glass of alcohol with his Jewish neighbour in the Leeds suburb into which he and his family had moved, an area not known for its large Muslim population.

Increasingly over recent years, particularly following 9/11 and then 7/7 and the corresponding assault in the media upon Islam, my friend returned to a more serious engagement with his faith. He wanted to have the knowledge to defend his heritage, and began attending mosque regularly and reading the Qur'an. He started playing recitals of the Qur'an in his café, instead of the contemporary rock, reggae and dance music he used to play, creating a peaceful, gentle ambience in comparison with the more noisy and busy feel of the café in the past. His beard has grown and he is determined to learn more Arabic so that he can read and study the Qur'an in greater depth. His suburban neighbours' reactions to his rekindled faith have not been positive: an elderly neighbour whose shopping he had done for years asked that another neighbour do it instead; people who have been friendly acquaintances have become colder and less willing to engage in idle conversation. He senses an unease, disapproval and says he is considering taking his family back to Kashmir to live. My friend is no extremist nor even particularly political; he follows the traditionalist Sufi path of many Muslims whose heritage is South Asian. But he seriously wonders what kind of place Britain will be for Muslims when his children become adults. He is concerned for their future.

This is a very concrete example of the effects of what has come to be known as 'Islamophobia', the irrational fear and prejudice towards Islam that is in much of our media and is behind the intense scrutiny that the Muslim community has faced from government and media over the last few years. We do not hear or read about the hurt and fear that is generated within the Muslim community by this or about the effects this cultural mood has upon the everyday lives of ordinary devout Muslims. My café-owning friend clearly displays hurt when telling the story of his neighbours. He cannot see why what he has rediscovered in the beauty and truth of his faith should be seen by others as negative and a cause for them to view him as a threat.

Then there is the hijab: this visible symbol of faith challenges the secular aim to privatise religion. Naila, a community worker in Leeds, told me how she has been spat upon and verbally abused in the street and on public transport for wearing her hijab. In this culture, Muslim women are criticised for wearing hijab and stereotyped as oppressed for doing so, whilst the complex motivations of a woman of faith deciding to wear hijab, or indeed to not wear it, are ignored or trivialised. The dynamism and leadership of many Muslim women of faith, on the ground in local communities and in the anti-war movement, is ignored or unrecognised.

We live in a culture of fear. We are encouraged by government and media commentators from the right and liberal left to think that there is something deeply problematic about Islam itself and that it poses a great threat to 'our way of life'. A *Financial Times* poll in August 2007 found attitudes to Muslims in Britain exceedingly negative in comparison with attitudes in other European countries. 'Terrorism' is constantly posed as a 'Muslim problem'; yet the rise of groups like Al-Qaeda is a complex part of geopolitical forces that have their roots in the cold war struggles of the '70s and '80s and in the foreign policies and covert operations of Western governments and intelligence, rather than something that is inherent to Islam. Indeed, genuine information of the phenomenon of so-called 'Islamic terrorism' is rare and most of what we hear about it from government and media sources is confused and contradictory.

In this climate, debate on the future of our world is stifled: anyone labelled a 'Radical Muslim' is considered a supporter of 'terrorism'. This catch-all term, which takes in many differing perspectives and groups, including those who argue for non-violent political struggle, marginalises potential contributions to the debate on the Middle East, global economics, international relations, Israel/Palestine and so on. Organisations with links and popular support in the Muslim-majority world are often dismissed, as they are labelled apologists for terrorism. An assumption is made that Islam needs to maintain a distinction between the spiritual and the political (something that most Muslims would see as absurd) to be accepted in Britain.

Media and politicians criticise Muslims for putting faith before nationality or patriotism, yet this is at the heart of a tradition like Islam, and indeed should also be so with Christianity, whose adherents are supposed to recognise a greater loyalty to and authority in God over and above any loyalty to or authority of a nation state. Such views are seen as suspect in mainstream secular political culture while they are basic to many Muslims' self-understanding.

It is the very fact that some Islamic groups bring religiously influenced politics back into the public sphere that is seen as so challenging to a secular politics that insists on a division between the spiritual and the political, and a wider secular culture that insists on the privatisation of religion.

We are rarely presented with positive and joyful images of Islam, yet this has been overwhelmingly my experience. One such experience was on a Friday evening at the beginning of a week of celebrations for the anniversary of the birthday of the Prophet Muhammad. My friend Assan took me to a large mosque in Bradford. The atmosphere was electric: many of the men were dressed in colourful traditional clothing, the smell of perfumes filled the air and I was greeted by many a passing stranger noticing my clerical collar and taking me warmly by my hand or greeting me with an open welcoming smile. When we finally managed to get into the main part of the mosque, after some simple food was served to us in the basement, I saw colourful banners adorning every side; ecstatic renditions of poetry to the Prophet were being recited and enthusiastically received by a congregation who exhibited a real sense of excitement, love and joy.

This book is a small attempt to counter the culture of Islamophobia. I want to share my real appreciation of Islam, telling stories of what I have learnt from my Muslim brothers and sisters over the last six years since 9/11 and how my engagement with Islam has deepened my own Christian faith. That engagement with Islam has been mainly in the context of being a parish priest working in inner-city Leeds. My parish had four mosques in or near it and was featured in the news following the London bombings in July 2005: the 'bomb factory' was discovered in a flat only 100 yards from our church, set up as a base by people who did not live in the locality. We believe it was the five years of solidarity work and dialogue as a church community and our strong anti-war witness prior to 7/7 that allowed us to play a central role in the community's response to this crisis. It is the story of that work of solidarity and dialogue that is outlined in much of this book.

The final section of the book, entitled Dialogue, opens a space for responses. Annie Heppenstall responds as a Christian woman in dialogue with Muslims; Hussein Mehdi, my companion on the journey to Iraq, tells his side of the story; and Firdaws Khan responds as a Muslim involved in the anti-war movement.

The rest of the book is divided into two parts. This first part, Solidarity, tells the story of our developing relationships with the Muslim community through our peace witness post-9/11, and offers theological and spiritual reflection upon that, concluding with my trip to Iraq post-occupation in February/March 2004. Part two, Truth, keeps with the style of reflection inspired by story, but concentrates more on questions of theological interpretation between the two traditions of Islam and Christianity. Dialogue is presented as something that, far from threatening one's Christian faith, can in fact deepen and strengthen it. I want to encourage other Christians to enter into a similar process of opening their hearts to Muslims, and to resist the culture of fear. This is a process that I believe involves us firstly in appreciating Islam, secondly in the repenting of our sins in relation to Islam and thirdly in witnessing to the truth as we know it in Jesus.

Throughout the book, truth in Jesus is articulated as a radical anti-imperialist and militantly non-violent Christianity that can join forces with Muslims and other communities to resist the increasing threat posed to God's planet and people by empire and global capitalism, and create spaces that reveal the truth of God's Kingdom, rooted in the unique vision of God that has been revealed to Christians in the life, death and resurrection of Jesus Christ. That vision, I feel, calls us to mould a faith-inspired or *Theo* politics that is motivated by love and compassion and visions of discipleship and action that are about service, radical vulnerability and suffering for the truth. This struggle, this *jihad*, does not allow us as Christians to reject the imperial road of our mistaken contemporaries and ancestors in the faith, only to replace it with a passive pacifism that retreats from the world, but calls us to a new Church militancy that enters the fray of the world's violence and oppression armed only with a trust in God and compassion and love for all God's creatures. We need to recognise that the struggle against empire and capitalism is a spiritual struggle that requires not the demonising of any of God's creatures, be they presidents or suicide bombers, but the liberating of all from the wiles of what the New Testament witness calls the 'devil'. As the Letter to the Ephesians proclaims:

Put on the whole armour of God, so that you may be able to stand against the wiles of the devil. For our struggle is not against enemies of blood and flesh, but against the rulers, against the authorities, against the cosmic powers of this present darkness, against the spiritual forces of evil in the heavenly places. Therefore take up the whole armour of God, so that you may be able to withstand on that evil day, and having done everything, to stand firm. Stand therefore, and fasten the belt of truth around your waist, and put on the breastplate of righteousness. As shoes for your feet put on whatever will make you ready to proclaim the gospel of peace. With all of these, take the shield of faith, with which you will be able to quench all the flaming arrows of the evil one. Take the helmet of salvation, and the sword of the Spirit, which is the word of God. (Eph 6: 11–18)[1]

Footnote

1. All Bible quotations in the Solidarity section are from the NRSV.

Chapter two

Christian jihad

On the morning after the 'bomb factory' was discovered in Hyde Park, Pat, a local resident and community activist, came out of her house expecting to see her Muslim neighbour in the yard, wishing her a good morning as usual. However, she wasn't there, and then Pat also noticed that the curtains of her house were closed. When she knocked on the door she got no answer. After some time, her neighbour finally arrived at the door. Pat asked her what was wrong and she said she was afraid that people would be angry with her, and that her neighbours would not want to know her. That same morning I went into the local school and was greeted by a mother in hijab with the words 'We are so sorry.' Gentle, loving Muslim souls who had done nothing wrong were afraid of people using the opportunity to vent their hatred; people who had no need to feel shame were feeling shameful. Meanwhile, George, a regular at our community café, had been evacuated from his flat in the same block as the suspected 'bomb factory' and was camping out in Kirkstall Leisure Centre. Confused and tired after an uncomfortable night, he wanted to know when he could get back into his house. Others who had been evacuated were staying with friends and family. Police and media descended upon the area – things felt tense.

It was Pat who decided something needed to be done. She headed for All Hallows, picking up her long-time friend Raihanna Ismail along the way, who had recently been appointed manager of the local multicultural centre. They and others arrived at the church and sat in the café with me and

Ruth, one of our community workers. Originally we had thought of having a prayer-walk on Wednesday evening and a peace march on Saturday, and the group of us had begun planning this. However, at 4pm the local primary school rang me to say that all the parents who were picking their kids up were saying that the church was organising a peace march that evening, and the teachers wanted to know if they could come! So Sandra, our other community worker, hastily got the Kids' Arts Club that was meeting that evening to make a banner.

By 7.15 about 80 people from all over the area, and from different sections of the community, were present. After negotiating with the police, we headed off, walking roughly the perimeter of the cordoned-off area. People came out of their houses to join us, and by the time we arrived back at the church the number had risen to 150! We marched under the banner of Hyde Park Together 4 Peace, and the children led us in a chant that became our slogan: 'Peace and Unity in Our Community'. We made the local news.

On Friday we went on solidarity visits to local mosques and prepared for another peace walk on Saturday, 16 July with a picnic in the park. As we had hoped, Saturday's march turned out to be even bigger, with some 500 people marching. It's hard to describe how amazing this march was – its diversity, its power; the sense of collective expression was beautiful. My prayer on the morning of the 13th – the day after the 'bomb factory' had been discovered – was that we would be open to noticing God's healing power at work in our area and co-operate with it, and sure enough it really felt like the Holy Spirit was blowing through Hyde Park that week.

The church became a place for meeting, an organising point for people of all faiths and none; we were thrust, pushed into the leadership of this sudden movement. We organised little but found ourselves at the centre of a collective expression of unity and solidarity in the face of the shock of how the 'War on Terror' had really come home.

A local minister of another church said to me that his prayer on the day the bomb factory was found had been 'Thank God for All Hallows': He said it was our work over the last five to six years with Muslims and on peace issues, work he hadn't always agreed with, that provided the basis for us becoming the place to which people turned in order to express their longing for unity. Work that had been going on for nearly six years, but that took on a special significance nearly four years before, on September 11, 2001 ...

September 11, 2001, a day of such global significance, also had an impact at a local level, especially for members of the Muslim community. A teacher at a nearby school told me how she had comforted a Muslim parent as she wept after facing abuse in the post office; another Muslim woman, who was brought up in this area of Leeds and had always considered herself a local, told me about feeling ostracised and 'like a stranger'. We put up posters in church: 'Islam is not to blame – war is not the answer'. As I had done on other occasions, I attended Friday prayers at one of our local mosques, and invited the Imam, Fateh Muhammad, to our Sunday Eucharist. I asked that he recite a passage of his choice from the Qur'an. In our discussion on Friday at the mosque Fateh said to me: 'People turn to God at such times' ... and I found myself wondering: *What God do they turn to?* As I watched television I was struck by the image of congressmen and women gathering together to sing 'God Bless America'. Some maybe found it touching. I found it ominous and threatening, particularly alongside Colin Powell's Declaration of War. And I was reminded of those pictures of fundamentalists in the Middle East, Afghanistan and elsewhere proclaiming jihad on America, misusing the Islamic concept of a spiritual holy struggle for their own limited political ends.

The God of 'God Bless America' is as much an idol and as much a tribal God as the God of the Islamic fundamentalists whom our media are so fond of portraying.

For the Sunday after September 11th, I chose the following reading from Luke's Gospel:

As he came near and saw the city, he wept over it, saying, 'If you, even you, had only recognised on this day the things that make for peace! But now they are hidden from your eyes. Indeed, the days will come upon you, when your enemies will set up ramparts around you and surround you, and hem you in on every side. They will crush you to the ground, you and your children within you, and they will not leave within you one stone upon another; because you did not recognise the time of your visitation from God.'

I had spent a lot of time preparing my sermon and praying about what to say; the congregation was larger than usual that day and I wondered how what I felt I had to say would be received:

The God we need to turn to is the One True God of Love and Mercy, the One True God that speaks through the Wisdom of all the Abrahamic traditions, and as Christians this is the God we see embodied in the Jesus we heard about in our reading this morning. A God who shares our emotion, who weeps and laments the destruction taking place. But a God who also presents us with a challenge. A challenge to stop the cycle of violence, a challenge to look deeper into the causes of the atrocities of last week; a God

who calls us to wake up, who embraces us in our tears and our
grief and our anger and says: *Take a look at the world from where
I am – I have been weeping for years – hear my voice in the cry of
all those who have been bombed, murdered and destroyed in the
world's hatred, I knew this would happen.*

In our gospel, Jesus is prophesising the destruction of
Jerusalem in AD 70, not as some kind of judgement on the people,
but as an inevitable consequence of the violence and hatred that he
seeks to challenge. And this speaks to us today. We are called to
turn to the way of Love, not out of sentimentality but out of necessity for the survival of humanity. And the way of Love calls us to
set aside vengeance and to open our hearts to the truth that last
week's atrocities were something waiting to happen – as one writer
put it this week: 'the wicked and awesome cruelty of a crushed and
humiliated people'.

The challenge God presents us with is to stretch our compassion, is to understand that the pain we saw last week was
inflicted by people who had been driven to hate by the pain of the
Palestinian people condemned to statelessness and the indignity
of second-class citizenship in their own land, where thousands
have been homeless for decades, where massacres have gone
unreported; a hate fuelled by the reality of the killing of civilians
in Iraq and Afghanistan through bombs and sanctions; a hatred
fuelled by the witnessing of the hypocrisy of the US government
in its financing of Bin Laden in the '80s, which has led to their
demonising of him now.

We are called to stretch our compassion to those poor lunatic
fools, driven mad with hatred, who could carry out such a waste-
ful and callous act.

Martin Luther King said in the '60s, at the height of the Vietnam War: 'The bombs that rain down in destructive power on

Vietnam will rebound in terror and pain in our own streets and neighbourhoods.'

At a congregational meeting a few weeks later we explored and discussed our feelings about the war in Afghanistan: people shared how powerless they had felt as public grief turned to talk of revenge. I remembered reading an article at that time by a Roman Catholic priest who wrote about the atmosphere in New York following the destruction of the towers; he described how people in their grief turned to one another: folk were talking on the subway, people were questioning why it had happened – and then George Bush made a speech that called for revenge and the mood shifted and turned ugly. We wanted to take up a different position to the rising tide of support for war on Afghanistan, to act together and as a church. It is important to remember how hard it was to be against war on Afghanistan – a tidal wave of sympathy for the victims at the World Trade Center had been cleverly ridden by reactionary political forces in the US and opposition was not anywhere near as vocal or easy as it would be a year later with the impending war on Iraq.

The meeting decided upon a press release and statement about the war. The statement committed All Hallows to supporting the Stop the War Coalition and to mobilising for the November 11th demonstration in London, at which we would hold a Eucharist in Hyde Park. It also committed us to a series of meetings under the title of 'Understanding Islam – Challenging Islamophobia', at which we would increase our understanding of Islam while deepening our connections with the local Muslim community. Speakers included representatives from the local mosques and other local Muslims. After the series on Islam was completed, we organised another series, educating ourselves about the current world situation with speakers on the United Nations, Palestine and Afghanistan.

The statement was well received in the local Muslim community. One of the mosques read out the statement at Friday prayers, and parents of children who attended our local playgroup wrote letters of support and thanks. The statement also gave us a profile in the local anti-war movement.

Some people at All Hallows were unhappy with our anti-war stance. In order not to mirror the silencing of opposition to the war in the outside world, we committed ourselves to making space for alternative points of view through structured discussion, and at the beginning of December we hosted a preacher, suggested by people who felt uncomfortable with our position, who put forward an alternative view. Three people, two in leadership positions, decided to leave the church. They had argued that we could raise awareness about Islam without being against the war. This appeared to many of us as half-hearted solidarity. It seemed to us that true solidarity required taking risks and standing with Muslims in opposition to war no matter how unpopular or off-message that seemed in the wider community. For some of us this time also began a re-examination of the gospels and Jesus's call to non-violence. Our anti-war responses were rooted in a number of senti-ments: some people had an instinctive pacifism, some voiced their opposition in more anti-imperialist and secular leftist terms, but very few of us, I noticed, rooted our opposition in the Gospel. It was noticeable, too, that many of those who came from the Muslim community to speak in our 'Under-standing Islam' series were far more articulate about their faith than many of us: we were challenged by how central faith was in the lives of our Muslim brothers and sisters and by how able ordinary Muslims were to talk about their faith in comparison with the average Christian.

I found myself engaging more deeply with the gospel and in the midst of the country going to war could not but hear, week after week, Jesus's opposition to war shouting out at me from the pages of the Bible. With some doubt and opposition to our anti-war stance in the congregation I longed not to preach about the war, truly; but each week when I came to look at the readings I was challenged to, yes, yet again mention the war! I found myself increasingly articulating my anti-war response in overtly Christian terms, finding that the largely liberal theological position combined with a leftist social analysis that I had mainly been influenced by in the past was lacking in its ability to seriously address the situation. I found especially that those in favour of the war who were liberal Christians often argued without even a token reference to their faith, and often in individualistic terms: 'People have to make their own decisions about this war and should be respected for that.' Yes, I thought, but surely that decision should be made in conversation with their fellow Christians and should be able to be rationalised and argued for from the perspective of faith? It seemed to me that if faith meant anything it must mean something in a situation like the one we were facing and the gospel must have something to say – I really felt that if we seriously looked at Jesus we could not countenance support for this war. But I was also deeply conscious of the dangers of self-righteousness, and as conflict raged in the world and minor disputes broke out in our church and someone was hurt by things I said and the way I said them, I found comfort in traditional concepts of sin and the need for repentance and how that starts with ourselves. Increasingly, it was prayer in which I sought refuge and inspiration. I found myself going to the mosque for Friday prayers more regularly, sitting at the back, legs crossed, watching the wave of surrender as hundreds of worshippers bowed down in submission to the God of compassion and mercy; and I sought to bow down in my heart as I recited the Lord's Prayer. But most inspiring of all at this time was when we went to London for the November 11th march; for here, in the Eucharist we celebrated before the march in Hyde Park, and in the breaking of the fast for Ramadan at the end of the march in Trafalgar Square, prayer and protest became one.

Julie Greenan, an activist at our church, reflected upon that day in her diary:

100,000 people – two whole hours for them all to leave Hyde Park, where the peace march begins. Where the towering puppet figures were built: images of death and destruction, made of camouflage and webbing, with bayonets and machine guns for limbs, skeletal heads; collages of mayhem and chaos.

Near Speaker's Corner, one small group from one small church in one city stacks plastic boxes to form an altar. The rainbow altar cloth later becomes their banner. Ten metres away people following a different path unroll prayer mats and begin their prayers. The groups carry out their rituals alongside each other.

We have wounded your love:
O GOD, FORGIVE AND HEAL US.
We stumble in the darkness:
LIGHT OF THE WORLD, TRANSFIGURE US.
We forget that we are your home:
SPIRIT OF GOD, DWELL IN US.

'Bush, Bush, we know you – Daddy was a killer too!'

Against this megaphoned chant, a strong voice begins to sing:

'All we are saying, is give peace a chance …'

People along the route smile, nod. A thin line of mounted riot police stand redundant. 'What do we want?!'

'Stop the war!'

Park Lane, Piccadilly, Haymarket and into Trafalgar Square.

Voices calling for a new way, bounce off colonial stone. The grotesque puppet figures hover and leer over us. One woman speaks of the anguish of the women of Afghanistan: they have no answerphones, no mobile phones to broadcast to the world their messages of grief, loss, horror; to let us know their last words of love.

Dusk in Trafalgar Square. Floodlit buildings of the British Empire. Beneath Nelson's Column, the muezzin sounds the Call to Prayer, before iftar, the breaking of the fast during the holy month of Ramadan. The fast that is kept in solidarity with those who have no food. The vast crowd stands in silence.

At the breaking of the fast, bottles of water and dates are passed through the crowd. Food is offered in return, which is immediately shared with others. It is a colony of heaven …

I would remember that demonstration for weeks to come, especially the experience of the Eucharist, where our usual Sunday liturgy took on a new depth of meaning in the context of thousands gathering to resist the violence of war, the group of Muslims doing *salah* near us, the crowd of people who gathered around us, some joining in, others just observing silently, and then later the experience of the *Adhan* (Call to Prayer) before the prayers at the breaking of the fast. Increasingly, I found myself reflecting upon how the Call to Prayer had come to mean so much to me.

Allâhu Akbar Allâhu Akbar
(God is Great! God is Great!)
Allâhu Akbar Allâhu Akbar
(God is Great! God is Great!)

ash-hadu al-lââ ilâha illa-llâh
(I witness that there is no god but God)
ash-hadu al-lââ ilâha illa-llâh
(I witness that there is no god but God)

ash-hadu anna Muhammadan rasûlu-llâh
(I witness that Muhammad is the messenger of God)
ash-hadu anna Muhammadan rasûlu-llâh
(I witness that Muhammad is the messenger of God)

hayya 'ala-s-salâh
(Come to the prayer)
hayya 'ala-s-salâh
(Come to the prayer)

hayya 'ala-l-falâh
(Come to success)
hayya 'ala-l-falâh
(Come to success)

Allâhu Akbar Allâhu Akbar
(God is Great! God is Great!)

lââ ilâha illa-llâh
(There is no god but God)

When I look at the Call to Prayer in translation I long to
stand with its bold statement against idolatry and its affirmation of the importance of prayer. But these simple words have

a spiritual depth that is beyond their plain meaning and beyond questions about the status of Muhammad. I hear in it, as it is recited in Arabic, the truth of the human condition and the truth of our world – the wonder of creation and the painful realities of our wounds and our violence. The *Adhan* felt to me at this time like a beautiful mixture of pain and praise; and in Trafalgar Square on that demonstration it summed up the beauty of the Islamic path of faith, the beauty of the history of a land like Afghanistan and the pain of betrayal of a tradition by zealots, the pain of the oppression of a people by outsiders from Russia, the US, Saudi Arabia.

The war on Afghanistan was soon proclaimed as won and the liberal[1] intelligentsia who supported it were in a triumphal mood. Christopher Hitchens wrote:

But if, as the peaceniks like to moan, more Bin Ladens will spring up to take his place, I can offer this assurance: should that be the case, there are many many more who will also spring up to kill him all over again. And there are more of us and we are both smarter and nicer, as well as surprisingly insistent that our culture demands respect, too.[2]

The following Sunday was the Feast of Christ the King – a feast day that proclaims that our allegiance is to the vulnerable God who is found hanging on the cross. Hitchens's triumphalism reminded me of how much anger and dispute was around. As I said, people had left our church because they thought we had become too focussed on anti-war resistance; others had joined us. Friends had different views about the war. There were many strong feelings around ... and I felt the need to speak about prayer, to speak about repentance, and about a prayer I had found increasingly helpful, the *Kyrie*. It seemed to me to speak of our need to submit to God's mercy, to accept the partiality of all our plans, gestures and protests and to open our hearts to mercy and love. It was a prayer I often found myself reciting in my heart in response to the *Adhan*.

The words of Jesus from the gospel for the day, 'Father, forgive them, for they know not what they do', stood out for me:

What is our refuge from the madness that surrounds us? Our refuge is in seeking forgiveness for the mess and pain that is our world. Our refuge is in seeking forgiveness for our muddled and confused responses to this war.

Whether we struggle to support the war or struggle to resist it, we can do well by praying the Kyrie:

Lord, have mercy, Christ, have mercy, Lord, have mercy.

When we read our newspapers and watch the television news: Lord, have mercy.

When we find ourselves in dispute with others at work or at church or with family, and hurt and confuse one another: Christ, have mercy.

When we march for peace: Lord, have mercy.

Our true peace is found in Christ and the knowledge that all our actions can and will be redeemed in the love of God.

It is on that basis that we feel we can and do act, a basis that must be rooted in prayer and repentance and never in triumphalism or self-righteousness. But it is also true that we fail often in our action to truly live the vulnerable love of God, and so again we pray: Lord, have mercy, Christ, have mercy, Lord, have mercy.

It is a constant process of prayer, action, repentance, prayer, action, repentance …

And this is what we share, we people of faith: prayer and a healthy scepticism towards all political strategies of right and left. This is what we share, we Muslims and Christians: that we must in the end trust only in God and that more important than marching is praying and that all our marching must be done in the spirit of prayer.

One day during this time I turned up at the little mosque where Fateh Muhammad was Imam to find him sweeping the stairs. He greeted me warmly, laughing at my surprise at finding him doing such a menial task. 'This is *my* jihad!' he exclaimed. Later over sweet tea and fruit he spoke to me about the true meaning of jihad. He told me of some words of Muhammad to his companions on returning from a battle in the early days of Islam, at a time when its very survival was threatened by aggressive opposition in the Arabic world. Muhammad told them that they had returned from the lesser jihad to the greater jihad, from the physical battle in defence of Islam to the spiritual battle of the heart to surrender itself totally to God. This greater jihad, the struggle to surrender oneself to the mercy of God, is done, Fateh Muhammad said, through the cultivating of humility and compassion in striving against the forces of ego, pride, hate and greed. The Islamic scholar and mystic Sayeed Hossein Nasr talks of this striving as the inner jihad residing in all the Five Pillars of Islam[3], and goes on to say:

Through inner jihad, the spiritual person dies in this life in order to cease all dreaming, in order to awaken to that Reality which is the origin of all realities, in order to behold that Beauty of which all earthly beauty is but a pale reflection, in order to attain that Peace which all people seek but which can in fact be found only through this practice.[4]

And it is to an inner or greater jihad that we Christians too are called – to deepen our relationship with Christ who is our true peace. Nasr's words remind me of Paul's words in Romans when he tells us that in our baptism we die to the world of sin and illusion and rise with Christ to new life and new creation; and of the words of the author of the Letter to the Ephesians:

I pray that, according to the riches of his glory, he may grant that you may be strengthened in your inner being with power through his Spirit, and that Christ may dwell in your hearts through faith, as you are being rooted and grounded in love. I pray that you may have the power to comprehend, with all the saints, what is the breadth and length and height and depth, and to know the love of Christ that surpasses knowledge, so that you may be filled with all the fullness of God.

The lesser jihad for Muslims is not exclusively about physical battle with the aggressive enemies of Islam but is about striving for economic and social justice too. And it is on the idea of the inner or greater jihad, this striving to deepen our relationship with God, that the outer or lesser jihad actions for social justice and peace in the world must be based. This distinction between the two jihads is a helpful one for Christians to explore. For Christians the greater and lesser jihads can be centred on the call to non-violence of the God of Shalom incarnated in Jesus Christ. The lesser jihad is indeed the struggle for peace and justice in the world, witnessing to the call of God running through the Bible for Shalom, for Jubilee, for social transformation in favour of the poor and the oppressed and against violence, but it is rooted in the greater jihad: the inner struggle with the forces of violence and hatred that reside in our hearts, no matter how much we claim to be pacifists, as Stanley Hauerwas says:

'I say I'm a pacifist because I'm a violent son of a bitch (sic). And I hate the language of pacifism because it's too passive. But by avowing it, I create expectations in others that hopefully will help

me live faithfully to what I know is true but that I have no confidence in my own ability to live it at all. That's part of what non-violence is – the attempt to make our lives vulnerable to others in a way that we need one another. To be against war – which is clearly violent – is a good place to start. But you never know where the violence is in your own life. To say you're non-violent is not some position of self-righteousness – you kill and I don't. It's rather to make your life available to others in a way that they can help you discover ways you're implicated in violence that you hadn't even noticed.'[5]

This struggle to transform our violence is achieved not only through the radical accountability outlined by Hauerwas but also through prayer and spiritual discipline which then informs, and ensures the struggle of the lesser jihad is rooted in a powerful sense of God. The Five Pillars of Islam are often seen by Christians as an example of works righteousness: Muslims, some Christians believe, are driven by fear to perform duties that win favour with God. This I have found to be a gross simplification, and one that fails to grasp the beauty and sincerity at the heart of Muslim practice. Of course there are differences with how Muslims and Christians see the relationship between God and humanity, but one of the strengths of Islam for me is this structured spiritual practice that is demanded not just of its clergy but of the whole *ummah*, or family of believers. I want to acknowledge the Five Pillars of Islam as a beautiful discipline and allow my Muslim brothers' and sisters' practice of them to draw me into aspects of my own tradition that may have been lost or marginalised and can be ways for me to open my heart more fully to the reality of God's grace in my life, challenging and empowering me to walk the way of Christ in my resistance to the world's violence and oppression. This is what Gandhi meant when he spoke of 'being the change you want to see in the world'.

Talking to Muslims about the Five Pillars of Islam made me reflect upon the pillars of my faith. Upon what practices and attitudes open my heart to the grace of God revealed in Jesus Christ; what practices and remembrances challenge the dangers of self-righteousness and triumphalism, of despair and hyperactivism in the face of the world's conflict. What pillars hold me steady in the face of the idolatrous demands of consumerist and militarist culture. My five pillars of peace, through Christ, are:

1. *Shahadah* (Affirmation of Faith) – I need to live with the conscious knowledge of having made my baptismal vows at confirmation: *I turn to Christ, I repent of my sins, I renounce evil*; and each evening, as I say the confession at Night Prayer, return to that knowledge that the mark of Christ is upon me, that in my despair at myself and the world I need only turn to him again. And every year at Easter we renew those vows, and prepare for this event through Lent.

2. *Salat* (Prayer) – We need to recover the Church's tradition of structured prayer. Over the last eight years, through my contact with Muslims, I have deepened my relationship to the Daily Offices, the prayer structure of the Church. This roots me in scripture as I recite psalms and canticles and follow the natural rhythm of the Church's year. Nasr talks of the discipline of *salat* in Islam punctuating 'human existence in a continuous rhythm in harmony with the rhythm of the cosmos'.[6]

It is the same with chants. I love the Taizé chants because of their scriptural roots and of how they become, like the prayers of the Daily Office, embedded in our consciousness to rise up in us at times when our own words immediately fail us in prayer; at these times the Holy Spirit gives us these words of scripture that we have faithfully committed to our hearts.

3. *Ramadan* (The Fast) – There is a long tradition of fasting in Christianity that needs recovery. Lenten fasting has all but disappeared. Personally I have found in recent years joining in Ramadan as a Christian a powerful spiritual experience. For me fasting opens my heart to the need to live more simply, to the need to deepen my relationship with God as I grasp my hunger and thirst for Divine love that I so easily turn away from through just slavishly following my appetites, or worshipping the many false gods of the modern world.

4. *Hajj* (The Pilgrimage) – The pilgrimage to Mecca is a pilgrimage to the heart of Islam; for the Muslim this involves a real struggle and effort. In the Eucharist Christ comes to us to reside in our lives, in our communities, and we are called to make a regular pilgrimage to receive him into our hearts through the journey of the liturgy. Regular Eucharist with prayerful preparation is another of my five pillars.

5. *Zakat* (Charitable giving) – Two stories from the gospels – the story of the rich young ruler and the story of the rich man and Lazarus – say to me that Christianity calls for more than charitable giving. In both stories it is the rich person's inability to understand how their wealth is built on the poverty of others, like the wives of Bashan whom the prophet Amos condemns, that is crucial to their fall. We wealthier Christians need to understand this. We are called to have awareness of how our wealth, our riches, has often been achieved at the expense of others and today at the expense of the planet, and to repent. For me a Christian *zakat* is about more than charitable giving: it is about developing a lifestyle

that is simple and raises our consciousness about our exploitation of our neighbours and all creation.

In responding to war, exploitation and violence in our world, we need to act for justice and peace; we need to resist violence but we need to do so in the spirit of prayer and spiritual discipline. Yes, we need to become a prophetic church but also a mystical one; yes, a church that acts for and thirsts for righteousness but does so through contemplation on the depths of God's love for all creation.

In these times of trouble and fear let us hear the call of the minaret, so full of praise and pain, and let us too fall into prayer:

Lord, have mercy, Christ, have mercy, Lord, have mercy ...

Footnotes

1. liberal – This refers to a movement within the secular liberal elite that argued strongly for the invasion of Afghanistan as a form of what had come to be known as 'liberal interventionism'. This was often backed by a vitriolic rhetoric that was clearly Islamophobic. This line of argument has developed and changed over the last eight years and its most recent form is explored in 'Islamism and the Roots of Liberal Rage', by Arun Kundnani, *Race & Class* Volume 50, No.2, 2008, p.40–67.

2. Christopher Hitchens, *The Guardian*, Wednesday, November 14, 2001

3. The Five Pillars were created to encourage the development of God, consciousness in everyday life; they are: the declaration of Faith, the prayers, the fast, the pilgrimage, charitable giving.

4. Sayeed Hossein Nasr, *Traditional Islam in the Modern World*, Kegan Paul International, 1987, p.3

5. Stanley Hauerwas, from an interview with Colman McCarthy in *The Progressive*, April 2003

6. Sayeed Hossein Nasr, *Traditional Islam in the Modern World*, Kegan Paul International, 1987, p.31–32

Chapter three

Resistance & Love

October 2002: One year on from the war on Afghanistan and the focus is now the impending war on Iraq. People at All Hallows are central in the formation of 'Leeds Christians Against War on Iraq' – we make a bold banner that reads 'Deliver Us, O God. Guide Our Feet In The Way of Peace'. After our experiences of protest against the war on Afghanistan we now place prayer at the centre of our resistance. We discover Christian Peacemaker Team reservist Jim Loney's powerful 'Litany of Resistance'. We add songs to the liturgy and publicly pray it at every protest in the months ahead. We step out on the day of action organised by the local Coalition Against the War for a lunchtime vigil in Leeds city centre. As before, during the protest against the war on Afghanistan, Julie Greenan from All Hallows reflected on our vigil in her diary:

Some of us were hesitant at so public a witness, so vocal a display of our, perhaps, tentative Christianity. But anyway – we stood on the City Art Gallery steps around the banner Leeds Christians Against War on Iraq, and began the Litany of Resistance with the song 'I will rock my heart till the walls come down'. Strong voices around me gave me heart to sing out, to speak out the prayers: 'From the politics of hypocrisy ... from the avarice of imperialism ... from the filth ... profanity ... madness ... blasphemy of war: deliver us. Guide our feet into the way of peace.' It may seem itself profane that this witness against the demonic waste of war and of preparation for war filled me with joy. But it did. Joy and tears. This opportunity to make a physical, public declaration with others made me feel profoundly joyful. Authentic, somehow.

People passed, some quickly, some more slowly; others sat and watched and listened. Someone shrieked that we were communists, as she ran past. They will call us communists and subversives.

Who knows what difference it made? Maybe something stirred. Maybe we were written off as just another breed of fanatics. But for me, just to do it was what mattered. To take that step on to the street. To come out. 'From the violence of apathy ... the despair of fatalism: deliver us ...'

The day of action culminated in a large demonstration outside Yorkshire TV, actually located in All Hallows parish. There had been talk of blocking the main A65 road out of Leeds, stalling the rush hour traffic in an attempt to highlight the slow but insistent move towards war. We gathered as Leeds Christians Against War on Iraq and sang and prayed the litany again. Praying the litany several times that day, with its powerful and challenging words rooted in scripture, was an experience of deep spiritual significance for me. I found myself reflecting on the witness to Shalom – God's true peace – the witness of the Hebrew prophets, of Jesus, of the early Church, and I felt a sense of calling to join, in my own little way, this train of witnesses that stretched from the New Testament Church through the ages and into our own times: the foolish witnesses for God's Shalom. And, along with others from the demonstration, I stepped out into the road and sat down to block the traffic. Police quickly moved in to attempt to remove me and I focussed on my sense of witness, as I sang in my heart the words of the African chant from our litany:

Jesu, tawa pano;
Jesu, tawa pano;
Jesu, tawa pano;
tawa pano mu zita renyu ...

(Jesus, we are here ... we are here for you.)[1]

Removed to the side of the road, I slowly and persistently returned to the middle of the road and sat down again. And again, I was removed and again went to sit down. A young woman police officer, noticing my clerical collar, gently told me, 'Sir, you do realise if you sit down again you will be arrested?' I carried on to the centre of the road and sat down again. The woman officer called out: 'This one is a third-timer, I need help here to arrest him!' Three other officers descended upon me and I was carried to the side of the road, cuffed behind my back and eventually taken to a prison van. I later learned that Rabina, one of my Muslim friends from Hyde Park, who witnessed the arrest, spent some time remonstrating with the police about how they couldn't arrest me because I was a priest!

I found myself singing Taizé chants in the van, but stopped when I realised that others had been arrested and might not appreciate my singing! However, the others shouted from their tiny cells in the van to keep on singing, and so I did. Later, John, from Leeds Coalition Against the War, told me how hearing the Taizé chants gave him strength, as they reminded him of teenage years spent at Taizé and connected the Christian faith of his past with his radical social activism in the present. In the van I remember thinking of what it must be like to be a prisoner regularly transported from court to prison, or from prison to prison, in this tiny confined space, hidden from the rest of the world behind a tiny darkened window. I prayed for prisoners who every day are transported in these inhumane sweatboxes.

At the police station, the Anti-War Coalition's solicitor, a member of the Socialist Workers' Party, advised us to take a strategic approach: the police were willing to offer cautions and we should accept them. The others arrested with me accepted this so that they lived to fight another day and avoided a record, and for them a caution meant nothing anyway. Fair enough, I had done the same in the past as a non-Christian activist when arrested for protesting outside the South African embassy in the early '80s. But I refused this time on the grounds that I could not as a Christian accept this proposal – to accept a caution would be admitting that I shouldn't have done what I did, and I didn't think that; accepting a caution would also be promising not to do it again, which I couldn't do, so in all conscience I couldn't agree to a caution. The authorities had arrested me because they thought I had broken the law, and if that was the case then I should be charged with the offence and face the consequences in court. This to me is the meaning of Romans 13 ('Let every person be subject to government authorities …'), a piece of scripture often abused by conservative Christians and wielded against Christian civil disobedience and non-violent direct action when lifted out of the context of chapter 12, with its radical reaffirmation of the politics of Jesus:

I appeal to you therefore, brothers and sisters, by the mercies of God, to present your bodies as a living sacrifice, holy and acceptable to God, which is your spiritual worship. Do not be conformed to this world, but be transformed by the renewing of your minds, so that you may discern what is the will of God – what is good and acceptable and perfect … Let love be genuine; hate what is evil, hold fast to what is good; love one another with mutual affection; outdo one another in showing honour. Do not lag in zeal, be ardent in spirit, serve the Lord. Rejoice in hope, be patient in suffering, persevere in prayer. Contribute to the needs of the saints; extend hospitality to strangers. Bless those who persecute you; bless and do not curse them. Rejoice with those who rejoice, weep with those who weep. Live in harmony with one another; do not be haughty, but associate with the lowly; do not claim to be wiser than you are. Do not repay anyone evil for evil, but take thought for what is noble in the sight of all. If it is possible, so far as it depends on you, live peaceably with all. Beloved, never avenge yourselves, but leave room for the wrath of God; for it is written, 'Vengeance is mine, I will repay, says the Lord.' No, 'if your enemies are hungry, feed them; if they are thirsty, give them something to drink; for by doing this you will heap burning coals on their heads.' Do not be overcome by evil, but overcome evil with good.

I saw my actions as being rooted in an understanding of the meaning of Jesus for Christians in the context of the 'War on Terror'. Jesus was a radical prophet who posed resistance to both Roman rule and the established religious authorities of his time. Jesus preached the good news of God's reconciling love, a good news that was not easy for those in authority to welcome but which was a word of liberation to the poor and marginalised. His challenge to the religious authorities of his time was a challenge to the institutional tendencies through which the liberating message given to the people of Moses had been transformed into a legalistic ideology which now oppressed those people and itself collaborated with the oppression of Rome. He spoke too against the religious 'terrorists' of his time – the

Zealots and others who sought to defeat the Romans by indiscriminate violence against Roman authority and ordinary Roman people. He challenged people to 'love their enemy' and to 'pray for their persecutors' – a truly radical perspective.

Jesus's call in the Sermon on the Mount, to shame the oppressor through non-violent action, was a creative response to Roman rule: 'If someone strikes you on the right cheek turn to him the other also.' Just as creative were his healings and his approach to the elitism of the temple, challenging the religious hierarchy of his time. These actions, aimed at political and religious authorities, were matched by a call to a way of life that was deeply challenging for individuals facing an oppressive and barbaric foreign power, whether they were rich or poor, powerful or powerless within the local social structure.

It was this triple challenge – firstly, to Roman authority, secondly, to religious authority and thirdly, to the prevailing popular culture – that led to his crucifixion.

The three-way challenge of Jesus is the challenge we face as Christians today and is the gospel we are called to proclaim. Firstly, we are called to expose US imperialism for what it is – violent and terrifying, in the grip of evil forces and not to be seen as a benevolent force. Pax Americana is akin to Pax Romana, in that it proclaims liberation and peace through violence and oppression, a violence that is waged through war and through a neo-liberal economic philosophy and the horrendously unequal distribution of the earth's resources – a violence of which we are a part. Secondly, we are called to push for renewal in the church and for our ecclesiastically-centred preoccupations to be cast aside in favour of a confident proclamation of a radical gospel. This will lead us initially to increasing marginalisation, 'irrelevance' and numerical church decline, but also, God willing, to a growth in discipleship. And finally, we are called to challenge the prevailing culture of violence, whether in the form of imperialism or its opponents. In our case that means facing up to the challenge of refusing to be dominated by calls for national security in the face of the terrorism of the oppressed, the embittered terrorists whose rage has led them to a hatred that refuses to see the humanity of the oppressor. It means resisting the temptation to side with the terrorism of imperialism, and challenging ourselves and others to walk the way of love. And, in response to 9/11 and 7/7, that means the challenge to place the search for justice for all peoples above safety, security and vengeance for ourselves and those 'like us'.

In Christian history two options have been open to Christians: a radical non-violence and various versions of a 'just war' theory. The 'just war' theory just does not hold up in contemporary context – modern warfare with its civilian casualties cannot be thus legitimised. In recent years, the church has been one of the last voices in society willing to support war, confining itself to maintaining a largely cowardly silence, a hand-wringing reluctant support, as it did for the war on Afghanistan, or mild-mannered caution in relation to war on Iraq. I have yet to hear a theological justification for war post-9/11. No one speaks of a 'just war'. I have heard many Christians pragmatically accept that there seems to be no alternative and so reluctantly support the 'war on terrorism', but I would maintain this is because of our lack of confidence in the gospel. We listen to our own fears and concerns for security. Who can blame us? It is a terrifying world. Fortunately Jesus does not allow us to get away with that and calls us instead to listen to him.

The ancient tradition of Christian non-violence has not disappeared and has been kept alive through the post-Reformation peace churches especially. But it has also been growing in the mainline denominations since 1900. There has also been a marked change in its interpretation, from rather passive, personalised absolutist pacifism to a more engaged militant non-violent perspective more akin to the politics of Jesus. The Christian component of the anti-Vietnam War movement associated with the Berrigan brothers, which has continued in the anti-nuclear Ploughshares Movement of the '80s and '90s, is a stunning example of this.

It was in this tradition – whether publicly praying the litany at demos, or sitting in the road in October 2003, or blocking Menwith Hill, the US Air Force spy base, to highlight its role in the 'War on Terror', or clowning as 'fools for Christ' on the anniversary of the occupation in 2005 – that those of us from Leeds Christians Against the War and All Hallows saw ourselves as standing (or sitting).

I was eventually released from police custody on bail without charge pending a decision from the Crown Prosecution Service. This seemed to take forever, and each month I would return to the police to renew my bail or to hear if I had been charged. The local newspaper had picked up the story and each time I appeared at the station they would turn up as well and interview me; each article was positive and gave a good deal of space to my own words, describing my motives and intentions. Sub-editors also had some fun with this news piece, using epithets like 'The Church Militant', 'Rebel Priest', and on my second appearance, when I still was not told whether I would be charged or not, the headline ran:

PROTEST VICAR FINDS THE LAW
WORKS IN MYSTERIOUS WAYS
O Lord, let us wait and see if I get charged ...

Eventually, in January, I was charged with 'Obstructing the public highway without lawful authority or excuse'. I decided to plead not guilty, influenced by Peter's declaration in Acts 5: the authority of God over the law of the land. My excuse, if one could call it such, for breaking this minor traffic law was that I was drawing attention to the potential breaking of international law by our government.

Meanwhile, we continued to protest, taking a small coach of 25 people from church to a local anti-war demonstration in Bradford, and then a larger coach of 50 to the national demonstration in London in February. In this amazing carnival of resistance to war our little group of Christians from Leeds struggled to find space in the throng at the beginning of the march to pray our litany, but pray it we did and were joined not only by other Christians but, as before, by Muslims, who prayed alongside us. Andrew Wingate, who was one of those passers-by who joined us, reflected upon this in his book on interfaith dialogue:

On the occasion of the vast demonstration against war in Iraq in February 2003 in London, it was a moving and challenging experience to see the Muslims with whom we travelled to London from Leicester dropping out of the vast procession to pray in a mosque en route. Even more powerful was the sight of Muslim men and women using abandoned placards bearing such slogans as 'Not in my name' as prayer mats. They prayed in the gloom in a very muddy, cold and dark Hyde Park after speeches had taken place, before getting back on the warm coach. We Christians had no such plans, but fortunately a group from Leeds invited us to join them, in the middle of the crush, as they recited a liturgy before we went on our way ...[2]

War is steadily approaching – despite the resistance demonstrated by the popular protests throughout the globe on February 15th, 2003. I am next due to appear in court on 19th March. War is almost inevitable now and we await the announcement of the beginning of the bombing of Baghdad. I am in court for the setting of a trial date and to formally enter my plea. Because of the media publicity and the political nature of the case, my rather minor offence, which would normally be dealt with by magistrates, is to be heard by a District Judge. I appear before a judge to enter my plea. We feel impelled to not remain silent in this public space as our country hurtles towards war.

Twenty people from church and Leeds Christians Against the War are present in the public gallery. When it comes to the time for me to stand to hear the announcement of my trial date, I kneel instead, as planned, and make the following statement:

'Rather than stand before you, I prefer to kneel, not to the authority of this court, but to the authority of God, who is the Creator of the universe and the lover of our souls. I call on us all here to kneel either physically or in our hearts before God, and to join with me in prayer at this time of crisis in our world. Let us pray for the people of Iraq, that they may know the love and mercy of God as bombs rain down on their land and homes. And let us pray for forgiveness and mercy on our nation as it takes part in a blasphemous, immoral and criminal war. From the demonic waste of war and of preparation for war: Good Lord, deliver us.'

I then begin to sing a *kyrie*, joined by friends in the public gallery who have unfurled our banner, and someone from All

Hallows reads out the poem 'Arguments Against the Bombing' by Lisa Suhair Majaj:

> *consider the infinite fragility of an infant's skull*
> *how the bones lie soft and open*
> *only time knitting them shut*
>
> *consider a delicate porcelain bowl*
> *how it crushes under a single blow*
> *– in one moment whole years disappear*
>
> *consider that beneath the din of explosions*
> *no song can be heard*
> *no cry*
>
> *consider your own sky on fire*
> *your name erased*
> *your children's lives 'a price worth paying'*
>
> *consider the faces you do not see*
> *the eyes you refuse to meet*
> *'collateral damage'*
>
> *how in these words*
> *the world cracks open*[3]

We are ejected from the court and gather outside in a circle to pray the Lord's Prayer – a young police officer arrives looking for the 'protesters', only to find a group of Christians in prayer. We hand out our press statement to journalists present, which includes a description of our action along with the following declaration:

We must turn away from the evil of war and seek to promote life for all people. Our opposition to the war is rooted in faith and prayer. We condemn the evil perpetrated by the Iraqi regime, but we also hold to account the imperialist structures that inflict the daily violence of poverty and injustice on oppressed people throughout the world and are promoting a culture of fear. War is not the answer. It is barbarism. Violence will never overcome violence. We must outlaw the very notion of war, and channel all our energy and ingenuity towards militant non-violence, in the tradition of Jesus and Gandhi. We must find ways to act not from fear but from love.

It is in May that I eventually come to trial before District Judge Michael Wood. The Prosecuting Solicitor is Mehran Nassiri, a Muslim – and during his cross-examination we have an interesting theological debate about whether I can claim to act on a higher authority. However, when my solicitor, Ruth Bundy, calls Iona Community member and Professor of Theology at Exeter University Tim Gorringe as my theological witness, the Judge rules this evidence as inadmissible, retires for 45 minutes, finds me guilty and then gives me a conditional discharge of six months.

When war breaks out, Julie phones me as televised pictures of the 'shock and awe' bombing of Baghdad fill our screens. She is in tears – I am in utter rage. Increasingly the daily marches in Leeds city centre against the war take on an uglier feel. Passers-by are less sympathetic: there is an increasing feeling that now that the war has started we should be supporting our boys and girls. Protesters appear increasingly desperate and angry. Some of us meet to discuss what we feel about this, and out of our discussions we organise a gathering at All Hallows called Resistance & Love. We hand out leaflets at the daily teatime demonstrations against the war:

Resistance & Love

a gathering of people against the war, for support, reflection, prayer and meditation

Wednesday, 2 April, 7.00pm
All welcome

Blessed are the peacemakers, for they shall be called the daughters and sons of God.
Jesus Christ

Those who are closest to Allah's heart are those who walk gently on the earth and when the ignorant address them as 'fool' they reply 'peace'.
The Qur'an

My heart is moved by all I cannot save:
So much has been destroyed.

I have to cast my lot with those
who age after age, perversely,

With no extraordinary power,
Reconstitute the world.
Adrienne Rich

Be the change you want to see in the world.
Mohandas Gandhi

As the bombs continue to drop on the people of Iraq and we continue to protest for peace, we feel a whole range of emotions: frustration, anger, grief, despair, hopelessness. We are vulnerable to certain risks – burn-out through hyperactivity, or exhausted inertia because of despair. We may act from our anger alone and allow it to become a destructive force, as we defiantly rage against the war, rather than a creative energy for resistance and hope. We need to acknowledge these feelings, support each other and act with awareness and real hope.

As a group of radical Christians we believe that it is important for our protests to be creatively non-violent and that non-violent resistance needs to be based on love and compassion for ourselves and other human beings.

As activists in the anti-war movement we have found ourselves grappling with the demons of hatred, violence and despair in our own hearts over the last couple of weeks, and feel the need for a space in which we can openly acknowledge this and support each other and pray/meditate/reflect together, seeking to keep our action focussed and rooted in love and compassion for our world and hope for the future, rather than hatred of the powers and despair in the present.

We want to open this space to anyone who feels it would be helpful to them. Our position on the war is rooted in our Christian faith, but we are also influenced by other spiritual traditions, including the Soul Force of Mohandas Gandhi and the Engaged Buddhism of Thich Nhat Hanh, and we welcome all people of an open heart to our gathering. You are invited to bring a contribution to the gathering – a prayer, poem, song, dance, scripture or other inspirational writing – or simply bring yourselves and your concerns and feelings.

I join with others to lobby at the weekly Stop the War group meetings. We argue for a silent march that concentrates on publicising the human cost of the war in a simple funeral-style procession with pictures and names of the dead, including British soldiers. After some initial resistance to this not being 'militant enough', a group of us is given the responsibility to organise such a procession on one of the daily protests. We meet one Sunday afternoon around a table in our café at All Hallows to plan. We decide to march behind a coffin with a lone drummer striking a single beat and carrying no banners, no placards and engaging in no chanting. We carry images of injured Iraqi civilians and cards with names of members of the armed forces who have been killed. At the war memorial we tie our black armbands and flowers to the railings and we read again the poem 'Arguments Against the Bombing'. The power of this procession upon passers-by is evident as we are watched in silence and an almost reverential hush. A woman cries out as we pass a bus stop: 'But what can we do?!' The only hostility comes from some men outside a pub who shout: 'Bomb Saddam!' Surprisingly the police go to challenge them. Policemen and women who walk with us are amongst the most visibly moved. It appears to me increasingly that unless we are actually going to put our bodies in the way of planes on their way to create havoc on the Iraqi people, this kind of symbolic witness is the only truthful Shalom witness available to us. I retreat from attending the daily marches of rage and pray for peace, for an end to the bombing for the people of Iraq.

I also find myself – faced with many people's sense of defeat and hopelessness – reflecting upon the meaning of Christ's resurrection as the beginning of the end of the rule of the powers and the arising of apocalyptic hope that Paul speaks of being deeply political. We can continue to resist, I reflect, by living in resurrection hope. I ask myself: Did I really think war was going to be stopped? And in all honesty I have to answer no. So why did I protest? To witness, is my answer, to witness to the truth of Christ's resurrection, to witness to the truth that Christ has defeated the powers of death and destruction, and calls us to join in the victory by living the love of God. As Christians we are seeking to find ways to engage in the politics of the world that do not demonise people – be they government leaders, dictators or terrorists – but highlight the ephemeral nature of the systems of power that take hold of individuals, these systems that, Paul announces, will disappear through the transformative power of God's love. And we participate in that transformative process of God's love when we loose the systems' power on us by seeking to live the reality of our baptism by stepping into the resurrection experience of being a new creation – as Paul says: 'Be not conformed to this world, but transformed by the renewing of your minds' – we can become resurrected bodies witnessing to the truth of the victory of love by being willing to put ourselves on the line – to bodily resist the powers – to 'get in the way', as the Christian Peacemaker Teams say, by non-violent resistance, be it by marching, blockading, reconciling or getting on our knees and praying.

An interesting collection of people join our gathering of Resistance & Love – people share stories, readings from Christian, Muslim, Buddhist scriptures, poetry and song. Nicola, an occasional attender at All Hallows, said of the event: 'I was very moved by people's contributions and at the end had the feeling that hope was the tangible result – together, now, we are "hope". I guess hope is what is created out of the chaos of our personal responses – "more than the sum of the parts". The power of a gathering like this evening, I can believe in – I believe it is a radical act that says "No".'

At this gathering we meet Hussein and Muneer, Iraqi Shi'a Muslims; members of their families disappeared in 1980s' Iraq, most probably tortured and murdered by the then US/UK-backed Saddam-led Baathist regime. They have mixed feelings about the war: they hate the idea of occupation by outside forces, particularly ones that were so silent during Saddam's most brutal and powerful years, but wonder if its the only way to get rid of Saddam, who has caused their people so much pain and suffering. They become our friends and we commit ourselves to helping them in their search for their family members and the thousands of others like them. Phil, our website manager, helps Hussein to set up an online petition calling for the occupation forces to put resources into helping to find and recover the bodies of those buried in mass graves. The appeal falls on deaf ears as the occupation of Iraq begins, and no plans for such projects appear to be on the occupation authority's agenda. I am left with a lot of questions about how to proceed as a Christian in relation to resistance to this war and the invasion of Iraq. Developing relationships with Iraqis appears to be a good idea, and a small number of us begin to attend some events at the Ahlul Bayt Islamic Centre, a Shi'a mosque in a neighbouring parish where Hussein and Muneer's community of faith gather.

Footnotes

1. Jesu, tawa pano – words and music © 1990 Patrick Matsikenyiri, *Many and Great: Songs of the World Church, Volume 1*, edited and arranged by John L. Bell, Wild Goose Publications, 1990

2. Andrew Wingate, *Celebrating Difference, Staying Faithful*, Darton, Longman & Todd, 2005, p.18

3. 'Arguments Against the Bombing', by Lisa Suhair Majaj, *Al Jadid*, Winter 1998

Chapter four

A heart broken open

It is January 2007 and I am sitting in my Arabic class. Today my teacher Abir does not wear her usual colourful hijab but is dressed in black. She is so noticeably different from the other Muslim women present, who all wear the usual variety of bright traditional dress, and I am reminded that today is 10th Muharram, Ashura, and that for Abir, a Shi'a, this is a day of mourning ...

It is February 2005, and I am standing in our church playing host to an event organised by some Turkish Sunni Muslim friends. It is 10th of Muharram, Ashura. But the mood is not one of mourning but of celebration. It feels strange to me, as these friends share their understanding of the story of the Flood, and the Anatolian Muslim tradition of eating, on this day, a dish called 'Noah's Pudding', believed to have been first made from the last bits of food remaining on the ark. We hear also a vast list of celebratory commemorations that are allotted to this day by Sunni tradition. It seems strange to me, because it is only a year ago that I was in Karbala, Iraq, with millions of other pilgrims, commemorating with the Shi'a the martyrdom of Imam Hussein, in a spirit of deep religious lamentation and political struggle.

The differences in approach to this event in the history of Islam are significant and they highlight the difference between Shi'a and Sunni Islam, often portrayed as a political difference that developed doctrinal import by Sunni and non-Muslims alike. But for Shi'a, the difference between the two sects lies at the heart of what it means to be a Muslim and to follow Islam.

The division arose out of the dispute over who was to succeed Muhammad as leader of the Muslim community. The Shi'a believe that Ali, who was married to Muhammad's daughter Fatima, had been appointed by the Prophet himself before his death; whilst the Sunnis believe that the leader of the community was to be determined by a process of decision in the community. As the Prophet's family gathered around his deathbed, the tribes met and selected Abu Bakr as Caliph. Although supporters of Ali were discontented by the slight, Ali accepted Abu Bakr's leadership, and also the appointment of Umar as Second Caliph on Abu Bakr's death. However, when Uthman was appointed over Ali upon Umar's death, there was increased discontent. Uthman was eventually assassinated, and Ali at last was appointed Caliph. However, a movement centring on the Prophet's youngest wife and Abu Bakr's fiery and, according to Sunni traditions, learned daughter A'isha claimed that Ali was involved in the assassination of Uthman. A civil war ensued. Ali won, and banished A'isha to Medina. Ali was then challenged by Mu'awiya. Ali sought arbitration to resolve the dispute, but was assassinated by a fringe element of his own supporters, and Mu'awiya became Caliph over Ali's eldest son, Hassan. With this, what the Sunnis see as the rule of 'The Four Righteous Caliphs', the golden age of Islam, came to an end. For Shi'a though, the corruption of the Caliphate and the turn to empire was inevitable because of the failure to follow the line of leadership determined by the Prophet himself, which they argue was affirmed in the Qur'an, Surah 33, verse 33.

Next, Hassan was killed; poisoned, Shi'a believe, by the leadership of the Umayyad clan, who now sought to establish a dynasty. On Mu'awiya's death, his son Yazeed inherited the

Caliphate to confirm this dynasty, and it was against this increasingly oppressive rule that Ali's second son, Hussein, sought to make a stand – despite massive odds against success. Hussein rode out to meet Yazeed's massed army with a small number of supporters and his immediate family, and it is Hussein's heroic defeat at the Battle of Karbala that Shi'a commemorate on Ashura. Shi'a believe that in Hussein's martyrdom and suffering, the truth of Islam lived by Muhammad and his rightful successor, Ali, is saved and lives on in the bloodline of the Imamate, the rightful interpreters of the tradition. Muslims are thus called to follow Imam Hussein's example of standing and suffering for justice and truth in the hope of the future appearance of the 12th Imam, the *Mehdi*, who will establish God's justice and peace on earth.

I don't want to fall into what many Muslims see as the Orientalist[1] exaggeration of the differences between Shi'a and Sunni, particularly at a time when imperialist aggression in Iraq and elsewhere in the Middle East has managed to ignite these differences into communal violence. But we would also do well not to fall into the dangers of a rhetoric of unity that is located in a denial of reality, as Islamic liberation theologian Ashgar Ali Engineer said:

The fight between Shi'as and Sunnis has assumed dangerous proportions in the Islamic world in general and in Iraq in particular. And this despite the rhetoric of ummah wahidah (one community of Muslims). The more this rhetoric is used, the more cleavages occur between Muslims. Of course this rhetoric is being used to hide reality through the cover of ideality. The Ideal is never realised, even not realisable and hence we need soul-comforting rhetoric. The more ugly the reality, the more attractive the ideal.[2]

But Engineer also wants to point out that at the root of each tradition is true Islam: much of the conflict that has ensued down the years has been a conflict between political establishments vying for influence and control. Engineer draws upon the work of Iranian Progressive Islamic revolutionary Ali Shariati, who claimed that this struggle was between the corrupt traditions represented on the one hand by the Ummayed dynasty in Sunni Islam, and on the other by the medieval Persian Safavid Empire in Shi'a Islam. Shariati argued that the genuine Sunni and Shi'a sects of Islam are both rooted in equally radical and true spiritual traditions that at their heart reject empire and stand for justice and freedom from oppression for the marginalised. Engineer says:

Genuine Sunnis are as much against what can be termed Yazidiyyat (an ideology of empire building on the basis of injustice and oppression) as genuine Shias are. Both can unite to fight Yazidiyyat. It is Yazidiyyat which brought the paradigm shift in the history of Islam. This paradigm shift from Khilafat to mulukiyyayat (from deputising the prophet to building dynastic empire) changed the very basis of Islamic society.[3]

The Shi'a remembrance of Ashura can be seen as a refusal both to embrace this destructive paradigm shift and to pretend it never happened. But Ali Shariati warns that the remembrance of Hussein's heroics and self-sacrifice must spur people on to live lives of justice and sacrifice. He differentiates between the ritualised remembrances developed by the Safavid establishment and remembrance by engaging in the struggle for justice and truth in ways that demand personal sacrifice. In both Shi'a and Sunni Islam the tension between the way of the political establishments and the true path of the Prophet and of Ali is very real; and the way to unite the two traditions of Islam, Shariati said, is for people to live the latter path and reject the former:

It is not sufficient to say that we must return to Islam. We must specify which Islam ... One is of the caliphate, of the palace, and of the rulers. The other is the Islam of the people, of the exploited, and of the poor.[4]

On my journey in Iraq in February 2004, it was very clear to me that it was the latter form of Islam that I encountered so powerfully in those I met.

And so to the story of that journey ...

It was just before Christmas, 2003 that Hussein Mehdi, with whom we had developed a growing relationship following on from the Love & Resistance event, invited me to join him on his pilgrimage to Karbala for the 10th of Muharram, Ashura and the memorial of the martyrdom of Imam Hussein, which he was planning for the following February. It also became a pilgrimage into the story of the sufferings of the Iraqi people under dictatorship, sanctions and war. It was a privilege to embark on this journey, a privilege to be asked, and it was beautiful in so many ways – beautiful and humbling – beautiful because of the depths I discovered in the Shi'a Muslim faith that touched me profoundly. It was humbling in the wonderful hospitality I was shown right across the economic and social spectrum, including from Hussein's now sadly deceased aunt Umfareed – whose friendly, warm, open face I will always remember – who, along with her son Muwafaq, his wife, Abeer, and their lovely children, Jasimine and Tamara, made us so welcome in Umfareed's once-large home in Baghdad: the home had been divided into two – half having been sold in order to survive the austerity of the effects of Western sanctions in the 1990s. It was in her home that I broke bread and celebrated the Eucharist on Ash Wednesday with the help of her and her family, who went in search of grape juice and helped me burn the palm cross I had brought with me for the imposition of the ashes upon my forehead. And I remember the hospitality of Abdulilah, who was a distant relative of Hussein's in Karbala, who took us into his sister's tiny home and moved us with his beautiful singing and poetry, while his sister fed us simple, delicious and carefully presented food. She had been forced to move to this house following the execution of her son, who refused to fight in the Iran-Iraq War. Abdulilah showed us the letter his sister had received that demanded payment for the bullet that was used to murder her child. Just one of the many stories I heard about the brutality of Saddam Hussein's regime.

When Hussein and I went to Iraq in 2004 there was much talk in the Western media about the liberation of Iraq, and so – as someone who had resisted the invasion, marched and indeed got arrested for non-violent direct action against the war – I went to find out how people felt about this so-called liberation.

It is true that one of the first things that struck me on entering Iraq was the immense sense of relief amongst those I spoke to (predominantly Shi'a) that the old regime had gone. But did this – as politicians at the time were claiming – amount to liberation? Salih, a teacher in Baghdad, told me off, in the way teachers do, for using the term 'invasion' about the US forces. He said to me: 'Mr Ray, do not call it invasion, it is liberation!' Contrastingly, Uraainib, whose brother was in an Iranian prisoner of war camp for 16 years, said to me: 'The Americans talk of liberation, anyone can talk of liberation. Saddam Hussein talked of liberation, liberation for the Palestinians, liberation for his people, but it was empty words. As far as I am

concerned, Saddam and the US are two sides of the same coin!'
Two very passionate responses to the language of liberation –
one claiming it, the other rejecting it.

The truth is that politicians, tyrants and military chiefs all
use the language of liberation very easily and for their own
purposes. But liberation for a people is a deeper process that
involves much more than the relief of the removal of tyranny.
It is both material and spiritual. It requires not just being rid of
a tyrant but truth-telling; it requires not so much 'reconstruc-
tion' and 'democratisation' as healing. It requires the building
of trust and the possibility of real hope, and it needs to arise
from the people themselves.

The language of liberation is something that is prevalent in
our religious traditions. In the same way that thinkers like Ali
Shariati clearly read Islam as a tradition that calls us to liberation from oppression, I read the Christian tradition as one that
speaks and offers liberation. In the story of Jesus Christ – in
his ministry, death and resurrection – we believe that we are
shown a God who is with the poor and marginalised. We are
shown a God who in the crucifixion faces the worst of human
violence and responds not with wrath and destruction, but
with love: in the resurrection we believe Christ offers us God's
love again. We are called to embrace that love and live it in the
world. We are called to seek the crucified of today – the
victims of injustice and violence – and to respond to the
complexities of the violence and pain of our world with love
and compassion; to identify with those who are marginalised,
and from that place to seek resurrection in real healing, reconciliation and hope. We live that hope now because we are
rooted to the future hope of the coming of God's Kingdom of
justice and peace – the *Parousia* – when, as Paul says, 'God will

be all in all.' For me Christianity is a spirituality that struggles with the realities of our world – its hatred, violence and confusion – and offers a way of redeeming this through meeting God in our active identification with the marginalised and in our refusal to use violence.

And it is this struggle with the bitter realities of life that touched me in my contact with the Shi'a faith in Iraq, and in the story of Imam Hussein.

Two often used Shi'a sayings sat with me during my time in Iraq and formed the basis of my meditation and reflection on the story of Imam Hussein in light of the stories that I heard of people's struggle against oppression and war. The first is from Imam Jaafar As-Sadiq:

'Every day is Ashura, every place is Karbala.'

When Hussein and I set off for Iraq, I felt very unprepared. We had received a good deal of attention from TV, radio and newspapers in Leeds, and we spent much of the last couple of days there going to interviews. I really felt that our time would have been better spent praying, and I felt I could have done with a couple of days of retreat for preparation.

When we arrived in Damascus we headed straight for the border, only to be refused entry into Iraq, so we returned to Damascus and took the opportunity of the delay to go and visit the Shrine of Lady Zaynab. Zaynab was Hussein's sister who was imprisoned by Yazeed in Damascus following Karbala – who spoke out about Yazeed's cruelty and Hussein's martyrdom. I was struck immediately by the shrine's beauty, and felt a real sense of the presence of God in this place of pilgrimage and prayer. There was a group of pilgrims there singing a beautiful devotional song to Zaynab. The singing was in a spirit of deep lamentation, and I was mesmerised by it. The singing got louder and more intense, and around me I could feel others being drawn into the orbit of the lamentation. I found myself reflecting on the journey ahead, remembering stories I had heard, reflecting on the disappearance and execution in the 1980s of my travelling companion's brothers-in-law, the mass graves, the wars, the victims of sanctions — and I wept. I felt my heart was being broken open by God for the people of Iraq – this was the preparation I had needed, and there was no place more appropriate than the Shrine of Zaynab. And it was here that the words of Jaafar As-Sadiq made sense. Iraq today is Karbala, Iraq today is Ashura. And this sense that the struggles, sufferings and sacrifices of the Iraqi people are the reliving of the sufferings of Imam Hussein and his followers became even clearer to me as we eventually journeyed into Iraq and began to meet people and hear their stories.

I met Bushra – a woman in her 40s, with such a calm and kind face, open and compassionate – who lost six of her brothers and her father in the early 1980s and still lives only a few doors away from a house that had been turned into a detention/torture centre. She was ostracised by family and friends, who were afraid of being associated with her. I watched this woman at the Free Prisoners Association listening to the stories of others; I saw her in her own home providing comforting words to a young man who was openly grieving over his brothers. I heard her tell the story of her family with dignity and power. I was reminded of Lady Zaynab, herself a woman who, despite the indignities she faced, spoke out with words of power and truth.

I think of the houses I visited – one of them belonging to my travelling companion's wife's family – that were turned into torture chambers. I think of the spiritual deserts that these places have become. Like Karbala, perhaps these places need to become places of pilgrimage. At the time I thought: just as Karbala, once a desert, is now a city that in its holy places speaks of a deep truth, so these houses should become places where the stories of the victims of injustice and oppression are not forgotten but honoured, and where the whole truth is revealed – including the truth of who funded and supported the regime that tortured, massacred and imprisoned its people.

I think of the story of Imam Hussein's daughter Rocqui'a, who, when crying for her father after the battle, was presented with his head on a plate. I think of her death soon after – the effects of such cruelty and abuse, her trauma; and I think of Imam Hussein's baby, Abdullah, who died of thirst, and I am reminded of the children of Iraq today: the street children I saw rummaging in piles of rubbish in central Baghdad, the children with cancer because of the effects of depleted uranium used in the 1991 war. I think of the child psychologist in Nasariyah who told me that she believes 80% of Iraqi children are suffering from post-traumatic stress disorder. I think of the record of the execution of a nine-year-old girl, found by the Free Prisoners Association in Baghdad ...

Every day is Ashura, every place is Karbala.

Wherever there is suffering and injustice, there is Karbala, there is Ashura. Whenever we listen to the stories of the oppressed, and honour them by letting them drive us to stand against injustice and violence, there is Ashura, there is Karbala.

The second inspiration for my thoughts on Imam Hussein comes from Mohandas Gandhi, who said: 'I have learned from Hussein how to be oppressed yet victorious.'

And I was reminded of Gandhi's words as I listened to Quays' story. Arrested on suspicion of being members of the

Dawa Party, Quays and others were held in a security centre in a suburban district of Baghdad in the early 1980s. Quays was severely tortured and had several bones broken. He revealed to us the scars on his wrists and legs from over 20 years ago. He told us how, after three days of torture, his hands were so big and swollen that it was almost comical. He felt so thirsty, but was refused water and was left in a cell to die. He remembers the horrendous pain in his body, the bleeding from his eyes and nose, his feet and nails. His legs were broken and his shoulders dislocated. He thinks he lost consciousness, and then felt that he was in the Shrine of Imam Hussein … two scholars came, one moved ahead of the other to lead the congregation in Noon Prayer. After the prayers, the leader invited him to come and sit beside him. He went over to him, and he was offered two bowls: one with grapes in it and the other with dates in it, neither of which Quays enjoys eating. He chose three dates, and at that point he regained consciousness, his thirst and hunger had disappeared, and he felt strengthened in his spirit, and able to remain steadfast to the end. The guard's attempts to recruit him to spy on the others detained with him failed. And it was his faith in God and the inspiration he drew from the story of Imam Hussein that helped him through. The story of Imam Hussein helped him to become victorious in the face of oppression.

It is the power of Hussein's story, and the effects that it clearly had on these people who faced so much suffering, that impressed me most. S. H. M. Jafri, in *The Origins and Early Development of Shi'a Islam*, argues that Hussein was aware that victory through military might would be only temporary, because of the inevitability of a stronger power emerging; whereas victory achieved through suffering and sacrifice is everlasting and leaves permanent imprints on people's consciousness, as it did with Quays. And this spirituality elicited in me sympathy, a note of recognition, as it echoed for me some of the power I experience in the redemptive story of God's work in the life, death and resurrection of Jesus Christ. I was also drawn by the stories of Hussein's concern for the marginalised. I was told the story about the black scars on his back. After he had been martyred, people asked about them. His son explained that these were caused by carrying sacks of provisions to the homes of widows and orphans. He had to do this at night in order to hide his good deeds from other men. This reminds me of Jesus's call in the gospel:

But when you give alms, do not let your left hand know what your right hand is doing, so that your alms may be done in secret; and your Father who sees in secret will reward you.

Hussein's suffering and sacrifice gives people the spiritual strength and encouragement to resist oppression, a will that is fed by the hope of the coming of the *Mehdi*, the twelfth Imam, when:

There will be no more fighting among the people, since the justice of God will rule and will remove any reason for conflict and warfare. This will be the golden age of peace and harmony, under the government of God.[5]

Again, this has strong resonances for me of the Christian tradition: the eschatological hope of the Kingdom to come, a Kingdom whose coming into being has begun, Christians believe, with the resurrection of Jesus Christ. As St Paul says in the first Epistle to the Corinthians:

But in fact Christ has been raised from the dead, the first fruits of those who have died. For since death came through a human being, the resurrection of the dead has also come through a human being; for as all die in Adam, so all will be made alive in Christ. But each in his own order: Christ the first fruits, then at his coming those who belong to Christ. Then comes the end, when he hands over the kingdom to God the Father, after he has destroyed every ruler and every authority and power. For he must reign until he has put all his enemies under his feet. The last enemy to be destroyed is death. For 'God has put all things in subjection under his feet' ... When all things are subjected to him, then the Son himself will also be subjected to the one who put all things in subjection under him, so that God may be all in all. (1 Cor 15:20–28)

There is so much violence in our world. When I look at Iraq today in 2007 and see the horrendous escalation of violence that continues day by day, I reflect on the misguided belief that violence, of any kind, whether 'terrorist', Iraqi resistance, militia army or occupier, can lead to liberation or healing, and I am reminded of the story I was given by a young woman at the University of Karbala after I had addressed a conference.

She passed me a letter written in Arabic. Through my companion, she asked that whenever I speak or write of Iraq I tell her story:

She wrote about her mother, who lost her own mother and sister and uncle, all of whom were murdered by the old regime. Her mother never recovered from this deep loss and was deeply depressed and disturbed for the rest of her life: the young woman felt that she had no mother. She wrote: 'It is easy to show when someone has been killed, there is a body that is dead. How do you show when someone has killed someone by destroying their soul?' She felt she experienced no love in her childhood, that her mother was absent – too traumatised, too destroyed, too broken; and she too had felt soulless, because she had not experienced love. Then, in her late teens, she was introduced to a man who was to become her husband. He showed her love and kindness and through this love brought her healing, confidence and hope. They were married and set up home together in Baghdad; then the 'Coalition' invaded and, during the bombing of Baghdad, her husband went across the street from their home to get some water from a neighbouring house, and a bomb dropped upon the building and he was killed. The man who had brought her healing and spiritual liberation from the effects of the brutality of Saddam Hussein's regime was now killed by a bomb dropped by those claiming to bring liberation from dictatorship.

It is too easy to forget that the bombs dropped from aeroplanes by states, under the so-called legitimacy of war and for the cause of so-called liberation, can easily be as indiscriminate as the bomb attached to a twisted soul who sees walking into a marketplace and killing himself and those around him as martyrdom or an act of liberation. Violence can never bring liberation or real hope, only destruction and death.

On our way back to England, we found ourselves – again because of border difficulties – with some time to spare in Damascus. Hussein wanted to go shopping for a present for his wife in the markets of Damascus, and as we wandered through the streets talking and remembering the last few weeks, we also shared our frustration at not being able to return home to friends and family. 'Maybe,' I reflected to Hussein, as we looked at shops, 'God has something else for us to hear, to discover before we return to England.' Soon afterwards we entered a clothes shop and were met by a friendly young man who, in the process of showing Hussein some clothes, entered into the conversation, realising that we had just returned from Iraq. He then told us that his brother had been killed in Iraq.

He was a martyr, he said; and he revealed to us that his brother had been the person who had driven the truck into the Red Cross building in Baghdad in 2003. Hussein and our new acquaintance had a long conversation in Arabic: this kind-faced man slowly revealed to Hussein that he was not very sure that his brother's actions were those of a martyr, and he told us that his family were not convinced either. He told us that his brother had a wife and two small children whom the family now cared for. 'Was he a martyr?' the young man asked Hussein. 'Or was he indoctrinated by people giving him a false belief in the righteousness of such an action?' Suddenly we were faced with the reality of the suicide bomber: an ordinary young man with a young family in Damascus, a brother who works in a shop, and a family who were left distraught and confused by his action.

How do we react to such stories? How can we respond as people of faith to the increasing insanity in our world and the continuing violence in places like Iraq? As a Christian I find comfort in Jesus's words that in the face of violence, wars and catastrophes we are not to be despondent or to speculate but to hold on to the truth of our faith (*Mark 13*).

Hussein went to the battlefield knowing he was going to die but knowing that victory in battle would not be any victory at all. Hussein was victorious because he won our hearts and we know his cause was true. Success in worldly terms is not necessarily a sign of victory, or of God's power.

Mother Teresa of Calcutta said we should all pray: 'O God, break open my heart so that the whole world may fall in.' In a world of violence we are called to cultivate compassion; in a world of self-righteous judgement and retaliation, we are called to practise mercy. 'Be merciful,' says Jesus, 'as your Father is merciful'; and as the Qur'an states at the beginning of each surah, 'In the name of God, the compassionate and the merciful.'

Compassion is a beautiful thing and it is only our turning again to embrace God's compassion and mercy that will save us in the end – we need to lament – we need to break open our hearts for the suffering in the world, for the victims of violence and torture and, yes, for the perpetrators of violence and torture, those twisted souls – be they powerful and ruthless tyrants or democratically elected presidents and prime ministers, or an indoctrinated young Syrian man with a family and a brother who works in a market shop.

It was a year after I had been to Iraq that I discovered Mother Teresa's prayer – it spoke to me of my experience in Lady Zaynab's Shrine in Damascus. There, God broke open my heart for the people of Iraq; there, God prepared me for my journey into Iraq; there, in that mosque, God met me, challenged me and spoke to me through the Iranian pilgrims' lamentation. I began to use Mother Teresa's prayer each day at the offices as a meditation, and over the weeks and months her prayer changed and I felt God spoke through the prayer, and my words changed from Mother Teresa's prayer to a sense of hearing God say to me, 'My child, I am the broken heart that lets the whole world fall in' – and the prayer revealed to me once again the truth about God, the truth about the cross. God is the broken heart. We have a God who breaks open his heart so that the whole world may fall in. As Paul says, this is foolishness to the intellectual and a scandal to the religious but this is the God that as Christians we proclaim.

In Catholicism there is the tradition of the Sacred Heart, a tradition of devotion where one calls to mind, through meditation on the heart of Jesus, his love for us. Ultimately, in his going to the cross, the path of Christ is the reconciling of God and humanity, the At-one-ment. The image of God in Christ as the broken heart that lets the whole world fall in became an image for me of the atonement – the glory of the cross. As a Christian I believe that Jesus broke open his own heart on the cross to draw all people to himself through his loving sacrifice and surrender, and calls us in that revelation of God's powerful self-giving love, which is at the very essence of creation, to do the same. To surrender ourselves to God's love and compassion, to prostrate ourselves before the one true God of love and sacrifice by living out a life of sacrificial love, mercy and compassion and creatively resisting oppression. That is the path, wherever we are, to true liberation.

Footnotes

1. Orientalist – A term used to describe a certain imperialist and Western disposition towards Islam in particular and the Arabic world in general, embedded in a particular form of scholarship and highlighted by scholars of Arab heritage like Edward Said.

2. Ashgar Ali Engineer, *Internal Struggle for Power – The Sunnis Versus Shi'as*, 2007, www.csss-isla.com

3. Ashgar Ali Engineer, *Internal Struggle for Power – The Sunnis Versus Shi'as*, 2007, www.csss-isla.com

4. Ali Shariati quoted in 'In Search of Progressive Islam Beyond 9/11', Farid Esack, in *Progressive Muslims on Justice, Gender and Pluralism*, edited by Omid Safi, One World, 2003, p.78

5. Ayatollah Ibrahim Amini, from *The Just Leader of Humanity*, Ayatollah Ibrahim Amini, chapter 11, translated by Abdulaziz Sachedina, www.al-islam.org

Truth

Chapter five

A Ramadan journey

It's not easy to let Ramadan pass you by if you live and work in close proximity to Muslims. It is not that Muslims go about showing off their fasting during the holy month; it's more that you notice a different pace of life, a different tempo. It is a month for reflection on God and a conscious compassion and carefulness in your dealings with others; for a deepening of spiritual practice. As one Muslim scholar says:

> *This month is a feast ... not of noise, but silence; not of banquets but restraint; not of forgetfulness but remembrance. This month is a feast for the faith.*

Coming into the Parish of St Margaret's and All Hallows in 1999, I quickly became aware of the presence of Muslims in the area and felt compelled to make friends and visit mosques. One of the things that struck me early on was this communal experience of Ramadan – how gently visible the practice is; and although I was not directly involved I found myself moved by and appreciative of the prayers and the fasting going on around me. Within a couple of years I felt moved to participate. At first I began on my own, quietly fasting for just one day in solidarity with my Muslim neighbours, then the following year for a week, then the year after that for the whole month. Then the next year again I fasted for the month, and also read an English translation of the Qur'an in order to try to understand the way of Islam more deeply. Over the years I began sharing my fast more openly with Muslim friends and regularly attended the special prayers at the mosques in the parish and broke the fast at communal *iftars*, which are gatherings for prayer and meal sharing. I also talked about my fasting with Christians, and learnt that others in our church had felt similarly moved by Ramadan. Elaine, who for many years ran the church's playgroup, which was attended by a significant number of Muslim children, told me how she too would often fast for a day during Ramadan. Annie told me of the eight years she had spent teaching in a school with many Muslim children, and how she developed a deep respect for and interest in Islam through the eagerness of the children to share their way of life. Isobel, a solicitor, told me of her discussions with a Muslim work colleague on fasting; and Peter described how he had always wished to write to Muslim friends during Ramadan to express his solidarity and thankfulness for the fast. I learnt how Hannah, who works with local children, would often get invited into family *iftars* on her rounds of visiting families at this time. As I shared my interest through preaching and discussion, others also opened their hearts, and began to develop their own ways of participating in the fast. Peter, Annie and I met regularly during Ramadan in 2005 to discuss our experiences. During Ramadan 2004 and 2005, Annie and I also developed prayer practices and wrote materials, including a pack, *Ramadan for Christians and the Christian Salah*, to help others in our church, and beyond, to engage with Islam at Ramadan. Over the years, the intention behind my fasting became clearer to me.

In 2006 – having spent the year developing contacts with Muslims around us and studying and reflecting on the Qu'ran – Annie and I were asked to address an anti-war group in Harehills, Leeds, who were holding a meeting on Ramadan. The group's main activists were young Muslim women. We simply

tried to share our positive spiritual experience of participating
in Ramadan, and some of our own Christian understanding of
fasting, and were deeply humbled and moved by their joy in
response. I thought of how much I had to learn from these
women, who daily proclaim their belief in God simply by their
dress, and face scorn and even violence for doing so. And that
opportunity to share and experience such mutual respect and
understanding was only possible because of the previous year's
strong sense of calling simply to go into the fast and experience it in humility and let it speak to me for itself, and then the
equally strong desire to learn more and to reflect more deeply
on Islam over the following year. There was a great significance for me about that journeying, between Ramadan 2004
and 2006.

During Ramadan 2005, I kept a diary of my reflections, and
extracts from this form the remainder of this chapter. I have
avoided the temptation of trying to construct a neat in hindsight
reflection on my Ramadan experience, instead simply offering
my diary extracts. So what follows is a day-by-day account of
my thoughts at the time. It does not aim to be 'theologically
sound' or scholarly. It is simply a record of a spiritual journey;
the inner dialogue of a Christian entering into Ramadan.

RAMADAN DIARY, 2005

DAY 1

7am

Well, I managed to get up, and had *Serhi*[1] of well-soaked muesli
and a pear and apple, cup of tea and pint of water. Started read-

ing Farid Esack's introduction to the Qur'an during meal that I borrowed from the bookshelf of Asim, the young Imam at the Makkah Masjid. Asim was at pains to point out that Esack, who is developing a liberationist understanding of Islam, was not approved of in traditionalist Muslim circles. At the time of *Fajr*, I attempted to follow the actions of the Muslim prayer, substituting the opening surah of the Qur'an with the Lord's Prayer and using the Beatitudes in the same way as a Muslim uses the shorter verses of the Qur'an, and using the Gloria at the time of prostration and the Jesus Prayer during the second *rakah*. Need to work out more of the details of this, including what determines the number of *rakahs* in a *salah*.

I then read the 1st *Juz*[2] of the Qur'an, which includes the first surah, considered the essence of the Qur'an, and a large part of the second surah, which is considered to be a summary of the Qur'an. It is considered to be a Medinah surah, and is concerned, it seems, with setting Islam in the context of the other Abrahamic faiths. I was pleasantly surprised that, although highly critical of Jews and Christians, it is in a rather defensive posture, in response to what seem like attacks from Christians and Jews:

> *Never will the Jews*
> *Or the Christians be satisfied*
> *With thee unless thou follow*
> *Their form of religion.*

Surah 2 v120 [3]

There are also some verses with powerful universalist (in relationship to Abrahamic traditions at least) sentiments. For instance:

Those who believe in the Qur'an.
And those who follow the Jewish Scriptures.
And the Christians and the Sabians.
Any who believe in Allah
And the last day,
And work righteousness,
Shall have their reward
With their Lord; on them
Shall be no fear, nor shall they grieve.

Surah 2 v62

My aim is to read a portion of the Qur'an each morning following *Serhi* and *Fajr*. I will do my Morning Prayer sometime between 8.00–9.30am, as usual, and then Midday Prayer and Evening Prayer before *iftar* and see if I have the energy to re-read the day's portion of the Qur'an in the evening again. I also hope to attend some communal *iftars* at the Grand Mosque and some of the recitations at Makkah Masjid at 8.30 in the evening. We'll see!

For me the purpose of participating is to step into the experience of Ramadan, concentrating not so much on the experience of fasting as a spiritual discipline, but upon Ramadan as a Muslim practice to explore the Qur'an and its meaning in Islam, whilst also obviously using the fast as a focus for prayer on world events and as a way of revealing and challenging my daily addictions, consumption and self-indulgence.

I have been struck in my recent readings by how Muslim writers make the (right in my view) point that the Bible and Qur'an are not comparable documents and are different types of scripture, in the sense that the Bible is not revelation for Christians – Jesus Christ is. So in entering Ramadan, a time for

Muslims of remembering and giving thanks for the Revelation of the Qur'an, I find myself wanting to look more deeply at devotional practices in the Christian tradition that focus on Jesus. I was just thinking of how the material we wrote last year emphasised getting into scripture – maybe a Ramadan for Christians should be more about concentrating on devotional practices in relation to Jesus? ... Getting closer to Christ ...?

2pm

Just spent some time in the café. Muhammad, an Afghan refugee whom I have known for the last couple of years, was in. His stomach is giving him trouble again. I say trouble but that is putting it mildly. He has a doctor's appointment tonight but he feels he will get no joy – he is really frustrated and upset: sometimes he can't eat for days as it makes him ill, but he still feels hungry. He was almost in tears describing how frustrated he gets feeling hungry but knowing that eating will make him ill. I am sitting here feeling hungry and a little tired, imagining foods, figs, fruit of all sorts and a cooked meal; I can feel my frustration bubbling under the surface, and I have a choice! Muhammad has a doctor's appointment tonight at 5.10. I can't go with him. I pray that the doctor will take time to listen to him and hear how upset he is, listen to his fears and try to alleviate his suffering. Muhammad fears he will just refer him to hospital for tests that could take months. He says he has felt suicidal at times but has agreed to ring me if he feels like that again.

4.45pm

Met R at 3pm, came round for a cuppa and a chat; I was feeling tired and hungry. He had so much to tell me and was quite angry about some of the things that have happened to him lately. As I was sitting with him I prayed the Jesus Prayer in my heart and found myself focussing less on my hunger and being drawn towards him. I felt able to give him more space and my concern with my hunger subsided. It felt a little like we ended up doing the Jesus Prayer together. He said how nice it was to just come and sit in the peace of each other's presence. He moved from anger to tears, tears of lamentation, which apparently happens after practising the Jesus Prayer for a while. There was a calm stillness between us. I prayed for him before he left. I felt blessed by the hour we had spent together.

8pm

Broke fast at appointed time with a glass of water, and remembered Jesus's words in John's Gospel that we use in the Baptism service:

> *The water that I give you will become in you a spring of water gushing up to eternal life.*

I could certainly feel the instant benefits physically. I sipped the water slowly and felt it work in my body; as I felt it quench my bodily thirst I gave thanks to Jesus for quenching our thirst for salvation, for a vision of love, truth, hope and beauty.

I was also conscious of Tariq Ramadan's reflection that I read yesterday, drawing on some words of the Prophet Muhammad:

> *The Prophet of Islam (peace be upon him) had warned, 'Some people only gain from their fast the fact that they are hungry and thirsty.' He was speaking of those who fast as mechani-*

cally as they eat. They deprive themselves from eating with the same unawareness and the same thoughtlessness as they are used to eating and drinking. In fact, they transform it into a cultural tradition, a fashionable celebration, even a month of banquets and 'Ramadan nights'. A fast of extreme alienation ... a fast of counter-Meaning.[4]

My friend Muneer talks of breaking fast with little food and not eating to excess. He talks of stories of the Prophet eating only dates and breaking fast with restraint. I decided to discipline myself to some figs and then prepare a simple but nutritious meal for myself and James, our church secretary, who came round to sort out the next agenda.

DAY 2

7am

Went to bed at 9.30pm last night so not difficult to get up; reminded of the words from Compline:

It is but lost labour that we haste to rise up early, and so late take rest, and eat the bread of anxiety. For those beloved of God are given gifts even while they sleep.

Continued reading Esack's introduction to the Qur'an. Esack quotes the Christian Islamic scholar Wilfred Cantwell Smith, who says the Qur'an for Muslims is *the eternal breaking through time; the knowable disclosed; the transcendent entering history and remaining here, available to mortals to handle and to appropriate; the divine become apparent* ...[5]

The way Smith talks of the Qur'an echoes how Christians sometimes talk of the Incarnation. Is it any wonder that

Muslims treat the book with such reverence, placing it on the highest shelf, keeping it well covered and handling it with care? How different to our battered and tattered bibles, with underlining and scribbles in the margins: the sites of wonderful contestation and argument of interpretation. How close to the Catholic treatment of the elements, in the understanding of the real presence of Christ at the Eucharist; touching, holding Divinity in the palm of our hands in the form of Book or Bread.

How different, too, though: the confusion of the broken body on the cross and the disorientation of resurrection, compared with the commanding guidance and assured authority of the spoken word of the Qur'an.

1.30pm

Presided at Communion at noon; of course I was strictly breaking the fast in Muslim terms by consuming the sacrament. But what a wonderful opportunity to open my heart more to the symbolism of receiving Christ in the sacrament. This is not food from which I am fasting, but an encounter that encourages my fast and what I am seeking to get closer to by fasting. Fasting is a spiritual journey not a physical endurance test. Catholicism asks people to fast for one hour before communion. I often unconsciously fast before Sunday Eucharist, maybe I should do it more consciously. There is something about receiving the sacrament into your body prepared, waiting, empty. Receiving into your mouth the sacrament where nothing has passed your lips for over six hours; when you feel physically hungry and know you are spiritually malnourished – *Jesus Christ, Son of God, have mercy.*

Saw Muhammad in the café afterwards; his doctor's appointment went well and he's feeling a little happier. We talked about Afghanistan and Ramadan when he was growing up. He also told me of how the Taliban would shoot people who weren't fasting; how people can so easily destroy something so good and true, something originally created to help people draw closer to God through peaceful submission and prayer, and turn it into an opportunity for violence and oppression.

7.40pm

Went round to see Mahroof at the little local Deobandi mosque around the corner; not had much to do with them in the past but wanted to hear if their application for building plans had been accepted. Anyway, we got into conversation about Ramadan and I told him I was fasting; he was pleasantly surprised and so I was invited to their *iftar*. Met some lovely people, mainly from out of the area, although I met a couple of locals I already knew. But after the preliminary *iftar* and prayers, as all the locals went off to family *iftars*, I was left to share a meal with this travelling group of brothers who are going around to different mosques and staying in the mosques giving talks, meeting people and learning from different places; some were from Huddersfield, others from Lancashire and others from London – itinerants really, quite a strange but lovely bunch – mixture of old, young and middle-aged – made me think of the apostles! One young man was very naturally friendly and was telling me how, although he was born a Muslim, he had not practised well and been a 'hooligan' for 'most of his life'. But now he was trying to follow the 'right path'. He couldn't have been more than nineteen.

It was strange breaking fast in community, as opposed to

yesterday's personal and prayerful breaking of fast; the Muslim experience of fast-breaking is definitely communal but also prayerful.

DAY 3

6.45am

Seem to be getting into a good routine of bed early, rise early. Feeling a sense of cleansing, sharper-focussed, less sluggish throughout the day. Even though hunger kicks in, emptiness seems less disabling than stress and overindulgence. Also not drinking tea or coffee probably helps, as well as no alcohol of course. Becoming aware of how much eating is a substitute for facing things, facing God maybe. This morning's reading from the Qur'an was interesting:

O ye who believe!
Cancel not your charity
By reminders of your generosity
Or by injury – like those
Who spend their wealth
To be seen by men,
But believe neither
In Allah nor in the last day.
They are in parable like a hard,
Barren rock, on which
Is a little soil: on it
Falls heavy rain.
Which leaves it
A bare stone.
They will be able to do nothing

With aught they have earned
And Allah guideth not
Those who reject faith.
And the likeness of those
Who spend their wealth
Seeking to please Allah
And to strengthen their souls,
Is a garden, high
And fertile: heavy rain
Falls on it but makes it yield
A double increase
Of harvest, and if it receives not
Heavy rain, light moisture
Sufficeth it. Allah seeth well
Whatever ye do.

It seems that the fertility that comes from submission to God is an inner growth, a strengthening of the soul. Really feeling attracted to this idea of submission, something I would have found oppressive in the past, but am feeling a sense of joy at the submission of my will to God, a letting go of control and a giving oneself over through practice of prayer, fasting and seeking more simplicity: *spending wealth seeking to please Allah.* This idea of submission in Islam is powerful and beautiful to me …

I learn more and more from Islam the need for submission (is this a male thing?), the need to strip myself of belief in my own power and control. I see that is Islam's gift – the call to submission:

If anyone desires
A religion other than Islam (submission to Allah)

Never will it be accepted of him; and in the Hereafter
He will be in the ranks
Of those who have lost.

As a Christian my submission to Allah is through Christ; I seek therefore an *islamic* Christianity. Christ, it appears to me, is the true Muslim, the one who submitted most fully to God's will. As St Paul says, quoting an early Christian hymn:

He humbled himself and became obedient to the point of death
– even death on a cross. Therefore God also highly exalted him
and gave him the name that is above every name, so that at the
name of Jesus every knee should bend, in heaven and on earth
and under the earth, and every tongue should confess that
Jesus Christ is Lord, to the glory of God the Father.

It seems to me that the call to submission is a call to peace. It is our desire for control and power – our desire to be gods – that leads to violence on all levels. It is the call to submission to God that is at the heart of Jesus's Beatitudes. The Beatitudes call us to let go of control and pride and to really be humble. To be empowered by a knowledge of God to whom we submit our desires for control, wealth and success and instead display the truth about our yearning for Spirit, our sadness at our own and the world's shortcomings and the seeming rule of death, our smallness in the great scheme of things, our longing for right to be done beyond political agendas; practising mercy, forgiveness, letting go. Seeking holiness, purity of heart where desire becomes wrapped totally in love rather than lust and power, and living in a way that by just being we are peacemakers in the everyday; and finally accepting as our lot, at best marginality, at worst direct persecution.

Blessed are the poor in spirit, for theirs is the kingdom of heaven.
Blessed are those who mourn, for they will be comforted.
Blessed are the meek, for they will inherit the earth.
Blessed are those who hunger and thirst for righteousness,
for they will be filled.
Blessed are the merciful, for they will receive mercy.
Blessed are the pure in heart, for they will see God.
Blessed are the peacemakers, for they will be called
children of God.
Blessed are those who are persecuted for righteousness' sake,
for theirs is the kingdom of heaven.
Blessed are you when people revile you and persecute you and
utter all kinds of evil against you falsely on my account. Rejoice
and be glad, for your reward is great in heaven, for in the same
way they persecuted the prophets who were before you.

DAY 4

6.35am

Yesterday went quickly and again felt an energy for most of the morning and early afternoon. Found myself praying the Jesus Prayer in my heart when going about things. Felt more open to interruptions and happenings. Slept for a couple of hours late afternoon, as I was going out in the evening. Didn't get to bed till 11pm, but managed to maintain routine this morning.

Again found myself drawn in reading to exploring the meaning of *islam*. Esack said this in a section I read this morning:

When I use the word 'islam' I refer to its literal meaning, a
personal submission to the will of God, the way it is most used

in the Qur'an. A gradual process of reification led to the erosion of the more pluralist understanding of the term until it was used as a rigid and formal religious system called 'Islam'.[6]

And this from the Qur'an:

O ye who believe!
Fear Allah as He should be
Feared, and die not
Except in a state
Of islam

Surah 3 v102

Today again I came across passages that are interesting in relation to the Qur'anic understanding of the other People of the Book and their revelations:

And there are, certainly,
Among the People of the Book,
Those who believe in Allah,
In the revelation to you
And in the revelation to them.
Bowing in humility to Allah:
They will not sell
The signs of Allah
For a miserable gain!
For them is a reward
With their Lord,
And Allah is swift in account.

Surah 3 v199 (my emphases)

This is the sense I've got from my reading so far: that this idea of *islam* as a way of being is universal, a point of contact between People of the Book and Muslims. There are those who practise *islam* and those who don't. The historical context of some of the surahs concerning Jews and Christians does appear to put Muhammad in a traditional Old Testament prophetic role: challenging the *Ahl al-Kitab* (the People of the Book), as the OT prophets challenged the people of Israel, to return to the original calling and move from unjust practices that do not show them as truly submitting to God's will. Esack points out that the descriptions in the Qur'an that say Jews and Christians have distorted their scriptures could easily be refer-ring *specifically* to the context of the Muslim communities' direct experience of particular Jews and Christians and their roles in politics and exploitation of the poor, and their claims to be superior to others simply because they were Jews or Christians. The distortion that the Qur'an talks about in the communication of the Torah and Gospel could be read as a deliberate misinterpretation and abuse of scripture in order to exploit and oppress, not as a comment that the scriptures themselves are inherently distorted.

Is this a basis for contemporary dialogue? The need for the Abrahamic faiths to act as prophetic correctives upon each other. How might this understanding help us to challenge misinterpretations of Christianity that promote the 'War on Terror' and Islamophobia? How might we present to Muslim friends and dialogue partners the challenge of Jesus's way of the cross that is not an imperialist attempt to convert others to Christianity but a gift to enable *islam*?

I was reminded in prayer this morning that I have been given the honour of being told by two Muslim friends that they consider me a Muslim because they see in me *islam*. I am far too aware of my own shortcomings and weaknesses to be able to embrace their compliment. But I thank God that in seeking to follow Jesus's way of the cross I have been able in the most inadequate of ways to show I am someone who longs to be a true follower of *islam*, to truly submit myself to the most gracious and most merciful Allah.

4.17pm

Just heard on the news about an earthquake in Kashmir – terrible and will affect people here, many of whom have relatives there. I sent an email to Asim on behalf of All Hallows to people at Makkah Masjid.

DAY 5

6.50am

Read this from Esack this morning:

> *(There is) an organic relationship between the Qur'an as written and oral text. This is an important point because most critical scholarship has focussed on the written dimensions of the text – without reflecting too hard on its message – and has failed to appreciate that its centrality to Muslims transcends this. Thus questions are raised by critical scholars about, for example, the identity of Mary as the sister of Aaron and the seeming discrepancy with Mary as the mother of Jesus without appreciating that the Qur'an is essentially evocative to Muslims and that it is often informative through its being evocative. In other words, comprehension can follow from the emotive and intuitive response that is evoked in the hearer and reciter rather than from study of its contents.*[7]

Attending some recitations as part of this Ramadan pilgrimage is therefore important – think I will go to recitation at the Makkah Masjid this evening and also take the opportunity to talk to people about the earthquake.

Need to think and write about this whole idea of structure and submission. Difference between choosing the structures freely in order to help you get the joy and beauty of submission to God and doing and living in the structures because you fear the wrath of God. In the first sense, when you step out of structures or stray, there is sadness and lamentation; in the second sense there is fear and loathing. There is a difference. I have found it interesting how I hear the references to Hell in the Qur'an; it's like I know the place: it's where I go when I really stray from the path. And I know the joy described as Paradise: it's that place where I operate from prayer which leads to openness and compassion for others without a sense of drain and resentment; it's the place I was at with R.

Today is Sunday and I want to concentrate on preparing myself for Eucharist; for receiving Christ empty, prepared and open.

DAY 6

6.30am

Just a quick note this morning as I have to go off to lead communion at the CSMV house.[8] Went to the recitation at the Makkah Mosque last night – went on for nearly two hours! Found myself just settling into it as a space for prayer. Not sure about the recitation, whether it was being done at a galloping pace. A bit like the galloping Masses some priests do. It would be interesting to listen to other recitations; will try to find some on the net. What was good last night was that some younger guys came up and introduced themselves to me, one of whom had read stuff on our website. Had a really nice conversation with him about fasting. He said how he had been fasting for 18 years since he was 12, and how he hoped his fast was much different now from what it was at 12; how abstaining from food and drink was not the fast, quoting what Muhammad had said. We talked about praying the hunger and recognising the little desires and addictions that get in the way of our relationship with God.

At the end of the sermon, Qari Asim read out the email I had sent to him about the situation in Kashmir, and pointed out to people that I was in the mosque, 'coming in friendship and solidarity'.

Only read a short bit from Esack this morning but read it several times as it was a very interesting point and relates to some of my reflections above, and will come back to it later on today. Esack was talking about the arrangement of the Qur'an and how it can seem incoherent and disjointed. Particularly in translation. I liked this that he said in response:

> *Because the Qur'an is the recited word in addition to being the written word, this seeming disjuncture is of little consequence to most Muslims. Repetitions are seen as God's repeated reminders, legal texts in the middle of a narrative as God drawing our attention to what has to be learnt from the text, breaks in a narrative reflect God's freedom from human literary patterns or suggest that the information contained therein is often incidental, while the mode, the sound patterns and inner rhythm are central. Most Muslims see the seeming absence of structure or classification in its surahs itself as*

*signalling a demarcation value and as reflective of the Qur'an's
role in the universe.*[9]

He quotes Kenneth Cragg:

*We are being properly divinely discouraged and frustrated if
we mistakenly endeavour to 'incidentalise' Qur'anic meaning,
to link what it is with when and where. We must needs follow,
in memorising, reciting, perusing and expounding, the
sequence of the surahs, serial and inward, as they stand in the
dissonance of dates, that we may better apprehend the music of
their truth.*[10]

There are questions for me here about the nature of revelation. Is there a link here between the poetry of God in the
Qur'an and the poetry of God in the revelation of Jesus
through cross and resurrection? Neither is confined to human
categories of comprehension and order: a looking beyond the
obvious, an idea of revelation as unfolding truth, an idea of
revelation as expanding our limited horizons.

DAY 7

6.55am

Took a bit of effort to get up this morning. It feels like initial
spiritual rush and benefit wearing off and now there is the
need to discipline oneself to sit in the routine and allow it to
work deep. The temptation is to give up because excitement of
new practice is over and obvious benefit hard to see. But it is
now that the time of testing has come. Just to live the practice
with no rush of new and amazing religious experience. Just to

submit in trust and love. As I find myself writing this I can feel how that submission itself is an amazing experience and how just getting up is loving God. It is responding to the call of our Lover: 'Arise my love.'

In my reading of the Qur'an this morning I came across a passage Muslim friends have quoted to me:

And nearest among them in love
To the believers wilt thou
Find those who say
'We are Christians':
Because amongst these are
Men devoted to learning
And men who have renounced
The world and they
Are not arrogant ...

It goes on:

And when they listen
To the revelation received
By the messenger, thou wilt
See their eyes overflowing
With tears, for they
Recognise the truth;
They pray: 'Our Lord!
We believe, write us
Down among the witnesses.

What cause can we have
Not to believe in Allah
And the truth which has
Come to us, seeing that

We long for our Lord
To admit us in the company
Of the righteous?'

And for their prayer
Hath Allah rewarded them
With gardens with rivers
Flowing underneath their eternal
Home. Such is the recompense
Of those who do good.

Surah 5 v82–85

I was reminded of the time in Lady Zaynab's Shrine in Damascus; when listening to the Iranian pilgrims' lamentations, I found myself weeping floods of tears ... There is something very beautiful and true about this *islam* and I cannot but sense a call to go deeper; and I cannot but feel that the call is the call of my crucified and risen Lord: it is he who calls me into *islam*, it is he who opens my heart to the Qur'an, it is he who takes me beyond the courtyard of difference to join in the wave of surrender in the heart of the mosque.

8.17am

Just read this from the Letter of James at Morning Prayer:

There will be justice without mercy for those who have not shown mercy, whereas mercy has nothing to fear of judgement ...

James 2:13

Forgive us our sins as we forgive those who sin against us.

We are called not so much to be good *but* MERCIFUL!

DAY 8

6.58am

I found myself really entering into a wave of surrender this morning when I did prayers after my meal; I found the Jesus Prayer just taking over and my movements becoming one. I was not concerned with whether I had said the right number, just moved as it seemed right, and it was the Jesus Prayer that cast aside all other words as I surrendered to my Lord.

5.39pm

Today has gone really fast. Been preparing for Sunday and looking at hymns, readings and preaching, developing a focus on creation and natural disasters. Thought I would preach on lamentation and love as a response to the Kashmir earthquake, using readings to explore the whole question of disasters and the God of love; readings for Week 3 of Creation season, that is, Joel on famine as judgement and Psalm 18 on God's anger like an earthquake.

In café tomorrow all day, covering for Sandra. So will have to use Friday to try to firm things up and possibly some of my morning space following Qur'an reading. So journal may suffer over next couple of days.

I was struck watching the rescue of a young boy from the wreckage of the quake last night – by how all the fathers around immediately shouted 'Allâhu Akbar' ('God is Great'), and by how I also heard one of them say about the disaster, whilst being interviewed: 'It is God's will' – a man who had lost family and loved ones. I balk at this as an 'explanation', but when it is said as a statement of trust in God, does that make it sound different? Does that make it different? Whilst intellectually I wince, I was moved to see this father in tears in front of the camera say, with all sincerity and integrity, 'It is God's will.'

DAY 9

9pm

Had great day in café, cooking, chatting with people – really enjoyed myself; must do a full day behind the counter more often. Really finding the fasting a cleansing and opening-up experience; seem to have more energy and am less sluggish, more motivation and more excitement. Sure I get tired but it's like I know why and follow my body more. It's as if I am more in my body, more incarnated, more aware of being a living temple amongst other living temples. Caring for my body and listening to it. Fasting does not feel like deprivation but detox! It's as if my body is welcoming the lack of excess and this sufficiency. Equally, the early to bed and early rising really suits me. But I need to stick to that – so I'll finish here!

DAY 10

6.53am

The reading from the Qur'an this morning was all related to booty and wars; a real sense of the context of this book came over me. I thought of the biblical 'eye for an eye' and how we Christians read that as a move towards non-violence, a move to limit violence. This morning's reading, whilst difficult and tedious, gave a similar impression: a real sense of struggling to articulate a 'just war' and to resist attempts to corrupt and undermine the fragile community of believers.

Surah 9 v24 speaks of the message, also in the gospels, that the community of faith and allegiance to God is often counter to tribal, national and familial loyalties and will challenge us to put at risk that in which we seek security in order that we seek nothing for security but *islam*.

I was also led to reflect on the universal nature of this revelation – it seems so contextualised at times, so limited to the time, so wrapped up in disputes – a common mistake made by people reading the Qur'an in translation. It has led me to reflect on the importance of the Arabic, the importance of listening to the Qur'an. Is the revelation the recitation, in the sense that the recitation takes us somewhere else, whether we understand the recitation literally or not? Or comprehend it when we do literally hear it? I have sat and listened to recitations of the Qur'an and been led into deep prayer and reflection. Even the other night, when the recitation wasn't great, I found myself praying easily and openly in my heart. I am reminded of what Kenneth Cragg said, quoted in Day 6. *[p.99]*

But also, the Qur'an does speak to our context and all contexts; for instance, there was also a quite hard attack on Christians and Jews. The one on Christians read:

> *... the Christians call*
> *Christ the Son of Allah.*
> *That is a saying from their mouth;*
> *In this they but imitate*
> *What the Unbelievers of old*
> *Used to say. Allah's curse*
> *Be on them: how they are deluded*
> *Away from the truth!*

They take their priests
And their anchorites to be
Their lords beside Allah.
And (they take as their Lord)
Christ the son of Mary;
Yet they were commanded
To worship one God.
There is no god but He.
Praise and glory to Him:
(Far is He) from having
The partners they associate
(With Him).

Surah 9 v30–31

It goes on, though, to set this in some context:

Indeed many among the priests
And anchorites, who in falsehood
Devour the wealth of men
And hinder them from the Way
Of Allah. And there are those
Who hoard gold and silver
And spend it not in the Way
Of Allah …

Surah 9 v34

There is clearly some serious corruption in the Christian Church that the Muslims have encountered, and they (and God?) are none too impressed. This led me again to consider: what witness do we give to the power of the message of self-giving love, when representations of Christianity that come over to the Muslim worlds are those of an imperialist expansionist emperor who claims God is on his side?! There is much to criticise in the so-called Muslim world, and indeed many Muslims are critical of it themselves, but these passages speak to me of the obvious effect that disloyalty to the way of the cross has on the possibility of sharing its true message. It's the log and the speck issue. Any disloyalty, any behaviour that shows us following any other path than the *islam* of Jesus is a log in our eye in the witness to Muslims about Jesus. This passage read with that in mind becomes a prophetic corrective to us today, as it should have been to Christians down the ages in encountering Muslims.

DAY 11

6.40am

Went to *jummah* prayers yesterday. Arrived early, at 1pm, and sat in the wonderful open space of the mosque; just a few old men praying or getting things ready. And then prayed in the silence and the space for half an hour while people began arriving. Nice that lots of people came up to say 'Salaam'. Asim, the Imam, began his sermon at about twenty-to-two. Much of it in Urdu, I think, some in English. He said the first ten days of Ramadan are for basking in the mercy of Allah: to bathe in the knowledge of his mercy that he pours down upon us. The next ten days are to seek Allah's forgiveness for sins: to acknowledge wrongdoing and seek forgiveness. The last ten days are to pray to be spared the fires of hell!

He also said that the one who offers fast without a true spirit faces God's judgement – fasting is not just abstention from food but abstention from wrongdoing, backbiting, violence, negative attitudes to others, etc. The fast needs protecting in order to benefit from it and not just turn it into an endurance test, and you protect your fast by your thoughts, by awareness and by your actions. He also spoke of the Kashmir earthquake. I think these were his words: 'Sometimes God sends calamity upon the Muslim people in order to give them a wake-up call to serve, to become humble, to turn to him.' God's mercy is so great, he went on to say, because if God brought calamity on all who sin we would all be caught up in God's judgement. The earthquake is showing us the power of God's wrath which, without his mercy, would destroy humanity.

DAY 12

5.02am

Got up and ate small meal and read Qur'an. But as today is Sunday only fasted until the Eucharist.

Meal with church folk and not eating again till *iftar*. As Annie said, it seemed wrong on reflection to be fasting on a Sunday, which is a feast day for Christians 'when the bridegroom is here'; as well as that, it would have taken me away from the fellowship at the meal after church.

DAY 13

9.31am

Just come back from walking Nelly and doing Morning Office – lovely autumnal morning. Felt a real sense of the rhythm of the Office this morning and how the words come up and go deep inside, but in a way that is not necessarily about literal meaning. Thinking this perhaps is similar to reciting Qur'an in Arabic.

This stood out for me from James 4:

Those conflicts and disputes among you, where do they come from? Do they not come from your cravings that are at war within you? You want something and do not have it; so you commit murder. And you covet something and cannot obtain it; so you engage in disputes and conflicts. You do not have, because you do not ask. You ask and do not receive, because you ask wrongly, in order to spend what you get on your pleasures. Adulterers! Do you not know that friendship with the world is enmity with God? Therefore whoever wishes to be a friend of the world becomes an enemy of God. Or do you suppose that it is for nothing that the scripture says, 'God yearns jealously for the spirit that he has made to dwell in us'? But he gives all the more grace; therefore it says, 'God opposes the proud, but gives grace to the humble.' Submit yourselves therefore to God. Resist the devil, and he will flee from you. Draw near to God, and he will draw near to you. Cleanse your hands, you sinners, and purify your hearts, you double-minded. Lament and mourn and weep. Let your laughter be turned into mourning and your joy into dejection. Humble yourselves before the Lord, and he will exalt you.

I like this and it is for me a connection to Islam. Luther called the Epistle of James an 'epistle of straw' and saw nothing in it but works righteousness. But that was surely a mistake. We have in James a Jewish-Christian text that is passionate for the seed of faith to bear fruit in action. There is no contradiction between Paul and James: Paul was tackling exclusivism and so is James. Paul between Jews and Gentiles. James between rich and poor.

It feels hard at the moment to 'protect the fast', in Asim's words, to not slip out of the spiritual benefit and fall into the endurance test. I have been reflecting on the individual and community aspects of the fast. For Muslims this is a really communal experience: families eat and break fast together and there are collective rituals and prayers for beginning and breaking fast. For those of us on the edge, Christians reaching out to Islam and wanting to bring the beauty of *islam* to our brothers and sisters in Christ, this is a lonely journey. For even when I visit the mosque and get such a warm welcome I am still 'other', and I feel my Christian brothers and sisters are not convinced of the path we Ramadan pilgrims tread. But I am also minded of the tradition in Christianity that calls for individual retreat, for Jesus's fasting in the wilderness. And the tradition of the Desert Fathers and Mothers, who retreated to the caves as hermits but lived in community, near each other physically but also in spirit.

DAY 14

I am finding myself called to go beyond Ramadan. This practice seems to really be what I am called to do. Will need to reflect on how this can be lived post-Ramadan. The need for early to bed and early to rise, the idea of studying early in the morning when my mind seems so open, the avoidance of excess and seeking to live with simple sufficiency, this is what is being opened up to me. How lovely and beautiful this is. This is *islam*, this is submission to God – and what benefits it offers.

Reading the Qur'an this morning, struck by how I am hearing it. Much this morning on judgement and heaven and hell. I find myself not balking at this but reading it metaphorically. There is something about abiding in God that brings a sense of the gardens of Paradise, the beauty, the peace, the knowledge of love and mercy; and there is a reality – and do I know it – of separation from God that is just a hellish self-inflicted shrinking of ourselves that brings bitterness to oneself and projects our own feelings of worthlessness onto others; a fire of recrimination and jealousy rooted in our self-inflicted separation from the love of God.

DAY 15

7.26am

Reading the Qur'an this morning I found myself in a similar mode to praying the Office. I was sat cross-legged on my prayer mat with the Qur'an open in front of me and I realised after a short while that I was rocking back and forth Jewish-style, as I sometimes end up doing whilst reciting the psalms. I also realised that my heart was sitting in the Qur'an, not trying to make sense of it, nor was I just mindlessly reading the words and thinking about something else. I was conscious I was reading the Qur'an and found myself just feeling a sense of love and gratitude for Islam. Reciting it was like the offering of this love, the love for *islam* as a path and Islam as a religion that I feel is Christ working in me.

I then found myself thinking of different people, as I continued to recite: of Muneer, my dear Shi'a friend with whom I love to sit and talk faith; of Hussein and our travels together, and from the same Iraqi Shi'a community, Dia, who always has such a warm embrace for me when we meet and whose family home in Iraq was used as a torture centre. Of the men of the Leeds 6 Muslim Council, so proud of the beautiful mosque they worked so hard to get erected, and which I love to visit; and of Raihanna, the manager of the multicultural centre, always seeking to build bridges between different sections of the community. Of the confident middle-class leaders of the Grand Mosque – passionate about their faith and expressing it in ways that seek to connect with the wider community. Of the late Fateh Muhammad, the old Imam at Makkah Mosque, and his powerful humility, and his young son who has taken on the role of Imam.

I was brought up short in this meditative reading by one of those passages that directly relate to Christ and Christianity:

Further, that he may warn
Those who say,
'Allah hath begotten a son.'

No knowledge have they
Of such a thing, nor
Had their fathers. It is
A grievous thing that issues
From their mouths as a saying.

What they say is nothing
But falsehood!

I found myself coming back to wanting to open myself to the challenge this passage presents. Is this another opportunity for us to look at how we have presented Christ's saving work? How we have talked about Incarnation? How we have presented the whole language of Sonship in such a way as to loose its meaning and reduce it to something that looks ridiculous and false? Is this another prophetic challenge to articulate the true depth of meaning and power in the relational dynamic at the heart of the doctrine of the Trinity and enter into serious dialogue with Islam on the nature of God? Is this an opportunity to listen to Muslims on God to hear the passion they have for God's unity, omnipotence and transcendence? And in dialogue, can we develop a way of describing, while maintaining Christian integrity, Christ's saving work that speaks to them a truth about God? What would a Christology developed in dialogue with Muslims look like?

10.08am

Just received email from Zunaid Karim at the Grand Mosque welcoming me to come to their *iftars*. I have also been invited to an *iftar* at the Ahlul Bayt Centre this evening prior to our Iraq Solidarity Fund committee meeting. Looks like the second half of Ramadan will include a few more *iftars*!

DAY 16

7.18am

Went to Ahlul Bayt Centre last night for *iftar* and prayers –
joined in for the first time! Hussein asked me if I would like to
and we did the *wudu* together, and he asked the Sheikh if I
could join in and he said he could see no reason why not. I
said I didn't want to offend anybody, but Hussein said that
people would just be more curious than anything else. He told
me that somebody said to him that surely I was a Muslim and
had converted. Hussein said in reply that I was not a Muslim
in the way that the person speaking understood it! I felt really
at home there last night, much more relaxed than say at the
Makkah, much more generally accepted – more than just
welcome. It's also very informal and wonderfully chaotic.

Saw Muneer too and Jassim. It appears as if the information
about me fasting and reading Qur'an has become an item of
news: I was asked by several people how my reading of the
Qur'an was going, how the fast was going …

By the time we had prayed, eaten, discussed, it was 8.30
and still the Iraq Solidarity Fund meeting hadn't started! But
the recitation for that evening had. A young man was leading it
and he recited beautifully; I closed my eyes and felt myself
back in Damascus, Baghdad, Karbala … and I felt the pull to
return. How or when I do not know but the sense of call was
strong.

I am heading off to my dad's today. I thought what I would
do while I was with him was try out a non-Ramadan discipline. So I will eat with him at normal times but watch what I
eat, and will still get up to study and read Qur'an and follow

my Ramadan prayer cycle. I also want to give the time I am down there over to him and when we are together make it space where I focus on him, without my mind being elsewhere. Honouring him, which I so often fail to do.

DAY 20

6.45am

Well, it's Monday morning and I haven't written in my journal since last Thursday. Went to my father's and followed the discipline of getting up early, eating and praying. Used the time between 6 and 9am to work on my sermon and then walked Nelly and did Morning Prayer. Then spent days with my dad. I ate a lunch with him on Friday but found myself living the sufficiency discipline and enjoying it. You really become aware of how much we overeat and how much we do so much to excess. As I was travelling on Saturday I had a coffee and some dates on the way home to keep me awake and give me a little energy. Didn't fast yesterday, as it was Sunday, and found myself slipping during afternoon and evening into snacking and felt quite full when I went to bed last night and didn't like it.

I also haven't been reading Qur'an since Thursday so it was nice to get back into the routine today.

Went to Grand Mosque *iftar* on Saturday night. I forget how young and multicultural the GM is. Met a lovely convert called Yousef and a Tunisian guy called Assad. Had some really nice conversations. I am going to return tonight and also go to the recitation, as Assad says it's the best he knows in Leeds. Again I felt drawn to join in the wave of surrender, but didn't. I would really love to be able to do this. In fact I would love to regularly attend mosque and participate in this as part of my own spiritual discipline. Need to think and pray about this more and look into working out what I am doing, a theology, a sense of keeping and developing spiritual and theological integrity.

I feel I put a lot of work into the sermon, as if it was a statement of the journey so far; feeling now a little like I need space from the writing and working things out.

But do like the idea of exploring the question: what am I doing by joining in the wave of surrender? Can Christians join in Muslim prayers with integrity? What do different Muslims say about this?

DAY 21

6.41am

Went to Grand Mosque again last night for *Maghrib* prayers and *iftar*; stayed around and met with Rasoul and Bilal, two more converts, and spent time with the mosque secretary as well as Zunaid Karim, and went with him and Bilal for tea at the café across the road from the mosque, before returning for *Isha* and the *Taraweh* prayers (the recitation). I joined in at both *Maghrib* and *Isha* and *Taraweh* and everyone was very happy for me to do so. Hassan was there also and very friendly and welcoming. There is something special about the Grand Mosque in how international it seems and also quite informal. Children run around the mosque after prayers, playing just like at the Ahlul Bayt, and there is the power of praying with hundreds of others joining in the wave of surrender, although I still feel a little too self-conscious. After what I said yesterday, it seemed silly not to join in.

The recitation last night was really beautiful and the *Taraweh* finished with some very powerful intercessionary-type prayers, almost charismatic, people crying the prayers were very lamentational – powerful stuff.

I am still forming answers to the questions I posed myself yesterday: something about crossing boundaries, something about openness, something about the call of Christ to dare to risk disapproval, something powerful too about loving the unloved. Everyone, including myself in part, is afraid, cautious, suspicious of Muslims; it's deep in our psyche; it's part of what we inherit; it's rooted in the 'sins of our fathers', so to speak. I want to give the message to Muslims that their tradition is one in which I find beauty and depth, challenge and sustenance, and I want to open my heart more fully to God who is known in the mosque and I want to know God more profoundly by allowing Muslims, and particularly *islam*, to work in my heart so that my vision of God expands and becomes fuller, truer. God wants me to receive and so I am opening my heart to *islam*; yes, as I said last week, I long to share, but I also at this stage just want to open my heart and allow God to give me what he feels I need to guide me on this journey and I feel Jesus/Isa is with me. Would Jesus have stayed out of a house of prayer? How can I enter into mosques where hundreds are praying to the God of Abraham and not join in? How wonderful to sit on the floor after prayers and eat and talk about faith with fellow believers. There is the importance of the integrity of my faith tradition but more important surely is acknowledging the integrity of God. If I believe in and love God, must I not also seek him in the mosque and through *islam* and indeed through those who have embraced Islam?!

Read this this morning in Esack, which really excites me in relation to dialogue about Jesus and developing the *islam* of Jesus idea as something that can speak to Muslims:

> Muslims in general deny the crucifixion although the Qur'an merely states: 'They did not slay him, and neither did they crucify him, but it only seemed to them as if it had been so ... nay God exalted him unto Himself and God is indeed almighty wise.' Elsewhere the Qur'an says, 'I am about to take you (Jesus) unto Myself and lift you toward Myself.'[11] ...
>
> Those who argue that Jesus was indeed crucified say that this verse merely denies that 'they' (i.e. the Jews) killed him and put paid to their boasts. The second verse is the basis for the notion that Jesus was lifted to God and that he never died a physical death. This may be difficult to reconcile with Q.5.117, where a conversation takes place between God and Jesus on the Day of Judgment and Jesus says to God, 'Nothing did I tell them, beyond what you ordered me to say: "Worship God, who is my Sustainer as well as your Sustainer." And I bore witness to what they did as long as I dwelt in their midst; but since you caused me to die, you have alone have been their keeper: for you are witness unto everything.'[12]

We come back to the Philippians hymn, which has an exaltation theology in relation to Jesus: *he humbled himself and became obedient to the point of death – even death on a cross. Therefore God also highly exalted him and gave him the name that is above every name, so that at the name of Jesus every knee should bend, in heaven and on earth and under the earth, and every tongue should confess that Jesus Christ is Lord, to the glory of God the Father.*

DAY 23

10.54am

Feeling tired and a bit jaded today. Got up for *Sehr* reading and early prayers and then read just one surah of Qur'an and went back to bed!

It's as if all the bright ideas, stimulation and inspiration have gone, have been stripped away and I am left with nothing but the practice. Strong urge to eat, to fill emptiness, but the fast helps me avoid this. Do I often feel like this and assuage it by eating? Is this not part of the journey?: going deeper beyond the excitement, inspiration and ideas to emptiness and boredom. There is growth here, learning, opportunity.

Walked Nelly in park very slowly. Going to keep a slow pace today. Have communion at 12.00; will take my sense of emptiness there and just meet Jesus with openness just to know he is on the journey with me. Simply connecting. Then will take communion to Doris this afternoon. Open to what that brings, less dutifully taking communion, perhaps giving it more time, seeking the quality of the encounter.

Today and yesterday been really empty of too much 'stuff', which is good; trying not to fill days with distractions or create busyness or feel guilty for not doing more reading or writing with the time on my hands. Just trying to keep a sense of God-consciousness in the space, returning to Jesus Prayer to hold me in; just trying to be.

6.46pm

Had a lovely day in the end, just following what came along; ended up having a full day but without a sense of knowing really what was coming next, if anything. Had some good 'pastoral chats' around café and through just calling in on a couple of people spontaneously when on my way back from taking communion to Doris. Ended up doing Evening Prayer on the hill at back of church with an amazing sunset – the opening lines never made more sense: *From the rising of the sun to its setting, your glory is proclaimed in all the world. Amen!*

DAY 27

5.30am

Had a lovely invitation to speak about my experiences of Ramadan to the Ahlul Bayt Students' Study Circle yesterday afternoon. Annie came along and I felt my talk was well received. Had interesting conversations with people afterwards. Felt very much as if my engagement with Islam and Muslims has taken on a real change this Ramadan. I feel more confident, feel less 'other'. Will go to congregational *iftar* tonight at Grand Mosque and must also revisit Makkah Mosque sometime this week. With all the clocks going forward yesterday my timings all out. Got up ridiculously early, at 3.45, thinking (because I had forgotten to change bedroom clock) that it was 4.45; anyway, didn't realise until after shower, so did Qur'anic reading before *Sehr* and have just prayed.

This great passage in the Qur'an this morning would have been good for yesterday's talk:

And dispute ye not
With the People of the Book
Except in the best way, unless
It be with those of them

> *Who do wrong:*
> *But say 'We believe*
> *In the revelation which has*
> *Come down to us and in that*
> *Which came down to you;*
> *Our God and your God*
> *Is One; and it is to Him*
> *We submit.'*

When I look back over my journal I realise that, quite understandably, it is these passages that stand out for me and upon which I have concentrated, the ones referring to the People of the Book. I think I would like to go over them all again and do some serious study of them regarding context and meaning to take further this idea of *islam* as a universal, but also to look at comments on Jesus and Christianity. I suppose what I want to try to develop is a Christology in dialogue with Islam, which might be termed the *islam* of Jesus, that is still within the parameters of Christian theology but presents Jesus from a Christian perspective to Muslims in a way that is fresh, challenging and interesting. But also simply because I feel attracted to *islam* as total surrender to God and because it seems to help me in understanding Jesus, and may also help other Christians to do so.

DAY 28

7.16am

As we draw towards the end of Ramadan: No great revelations, no real inspiration, just a settling into what has been discovered and how it might all come together. I think of the need to be fasting, and the need to take a similar attitude in relation to spiritual food to acknowledge sufficiency, to digest what has been given and to avoid seeking 'new' inspiration and more food when you have already been given enough to sustain you on your journey, to work with what you have. It's the way into discovering the depths of God in what has been given.

Footnotes

1. *Serhi* – the name of the meal before the starting of the fast

2. *Juz* – a way of dividing up the Qur'an for daily reading during Ramadan

3. The translation/interpretation of the Qur'an that I used was one that was given to me as a gift in my early days in the parish by some young converts to Islam who were working in the local Islamic bookstore, then called 'Rays of Light'. It was a very ornately bound copy published in Saudi Arabia, based on the translation/interpretation of Yusuf Ali, widely used by Muslims themselves; however, it is not a translation I use much now. For information on translations and approaching the Qur'an for the first time, see Appendix.

4. Tariq Ramadan, from www.tariqramadan.com

5. Wilfred Cantwell Smith, from *The Qur'an: A User's Guide*, Farid Esack, One World, 2005, p.31

6. Farid Esack, *The Qur'an: A User's Guide*, One World, 2005, p.47 (footnote 28)

7. Farid Esack, *The Qur'an: A User's Guide*, One World, 2005, p.56

8. CSMV – Religious Community of St Mary the Virgin

9. Farid Esack, *The Qur'an: A User's Guide*, One World, 2005, p.66

10. Kenneth Cragg, from *The Qur'an: A User's Guide*, Farid Esack,

One World, 2005, p.66

11. Farid Esack, *The Qur'an: A User's Guide*, One World, 2005, p.155

12. Farid Esack, *The Qur'an: A User's Guide*, One World, 2005, p.155

Chapter six
'Allâhu Akbar!'

I was watching the news at the time of the Kashmir earthquake when a boy was discovered alive in the rubble of one of the many schools that were destroyed. As he was lifted from the destruction, bewildered and frightened, all the fathers searching for sons cried out: 'Allâhu Akbar!' ('God is Great!')[1]

Here we were, at what was then, I think, the first week of Ramadan, and people were fasting, and this quake hits them, destroying their world – and still they are praising God! An interview with another father moments earlier, who had yet to find his son, saw this man in tears proclaim: 'It is God's will.'

Now, I have an in-built resistance to this as an 'explanation' of disaster, but I found myself hearing it differently; instead of hearing it as a vacuous explanation, I heard it as a statement of trust in God. I was shocked by how moved I was by it: I was moved to see this father in tears in front of the camera say, with all sincerity and with integrity, 'It is God's will.' I was certainly moved to tears by the cry of 'God is Great!' from the fathers as the boy was raised from the rubble, and was reminded of what Paul says in his Letter to the Romans:

When you cry, Abba, Father, it is the very Spirit bearing witness with our spirit that we are children of God.

The same week, I went to the mosque for *jummah* prayers on Friday and listened to the *khutbah* (sermon). The Imam, a young, gentle, open scholar, said of the earthquake, with a reassuring tone in his voice: 'Sometimes Allah sends calamity upon the Muslim people in order to give them a wake-up call to serve, to become humble, to turn to him.' Allah's mercy is so great, he went on to say, because if Allah brought calamity on all who sin we would all be caught up in Allah's judgement. The earthquake is showing us the power of Allah's wrath which, without his mercy, would destroy humanity. Our response, said the Imam, should be to pray and fast and seek Allah's mercy.

It reminded me of the attitude of many of the Hebrew prophets. Joel is an example: A famine has struck the country, and the prophet Joel calls the people to repentance through lamentation and fasting: *Lament like a virgin dressed in sackcloth for the husband of her youth … To you, O Lord, I cry. For fire has devoured the pastures of the wilderness, and flames have burned all the trees of the field. (Joel 1:8–19)*

Perhaps we read and hear such responses to disaster as unsophisticated and harsh, perhaps we see them as a form of belief that has long lost its usefulness; or we seek philosophical explanations to get God off the hook; or maybe we just give up on a transcendent, Creator God completely.

But I feel I want to caution against too quickly retreating from such responses to disaster as those of the fathers in the rubble, and the Imam in the mosque, and Joel in Judah, 300 to 400 years before Christ. For perhaps we read and hear such responses from a place that is quite rare in the human condition today and throughout human existence on this earth, a place of thinking that we are in control of the world and we can order and control our lives, and if God is around he is there for consolation alone or to protect us from being confronted by life's tragedy and disaster.

But I also want to move away from the need to explain in ways that point the finger either at God or us, from making too simple a correlation between our actions and disasters, too simple a connection between disaster and punishment. But I do want to learn from those fathers in the rubble of the quake, from the Imam's Qur'anic concern to maintain a belief in God's sovereignty, and from Joel's call to lamentation.

What do I learn?

From the Qur'an I learn the need to make God central – the need to hold on to an idea of God as sovereign Creator, as beyond our total comprehension. There is a danger of domesticating God, just turning God into a comfort blanket, devoid of challenge and anything we find strange and awesome. In my engagement with Islam I have been struck by its understanding of the Otherness – the complete Otherness – of God, and its concern to protect that understanding as central to its proclamation. This is not a sense of otherness that is the deists' absent God, but a God who is so present in God's Otherness that God is closer than your jugular vein – God is present to us in the signs of creation, in the beauty of the sunrise and sunset, and in the terror of the quake. God's signature is imprinted on the universe, as the Qur'an says in Surah Al Baqurah:

> To God belong the East and the West.
> Wherever you turn, there is the face of God.
> Indeed, God is infinite, all-knowing …

Secondly, from Joel's lamentation, I want to recognise the importance of a form of prayer that is passionate and emotional: the cry to God, the weeping over the earth's woes; the importance of mourning the suffering of the world, the importance of not avoiding the realities of the world and numbing ourselves through entertainment and addiction, the importance of not using other people's suffering to make ourselves feel good, or indeed bad, about ourselves – either by simply writing a cheque or turning it into an issue for ourselves: 'I feel so bad because I don't know what to do.' Lamentation is the alternative: not focussing on ourselves but turning to God. For instance, perhaps praying as we watch the news, simply and openly. We don't need to rend our garments or scream out loud. During Ramadan last year I was using the Jesus Prayer to develop my sense of God-consciousness; just saying the simple prayer 'Jesus, have mercy' over and over again – and it moved me from lamentation to love.

And from the fathers in the rubble I want to learn to have trust in God, to place God at the centre of my life, to respond to life's harsh realities with a genuine call of prayer, to recognise that my life is God's, that I am gift and my existence is because of God and God alone, to not only lament but praise, even in the midst of disaster.

The fathers' praise, a Qur'anic concern to maintain the integrity of God's sovereignty, Joel's lamentation are all rooted in living in a world where God is at the centre and prayer is central. This is what I want to learn – to place God at the centre of my life and at the centre of the vast expanse of the universe and at the centre of this fragile and awesome part of his creation, earth, our home.

But the cry of the Christian is not so much 'God is Great!' as 'God is love'. *'God is love, and those who live in love live in God, and God in them'* (1 John). For the Muslim, the important thing to understand is God's total oneness, uniqueness, God's Otherness, and God's power from which God exercises gracious mercy upon humanity. For us, God's transcendence has to be rooted in his love – love comes before power – God's power is his love.

There is a tradition of interpretation of the Hebrew Bible

that calls us not to see natural disasters as God's punishment. It highlights the story of Noah, a story also found, with significant differences, in the Qur'an. In the Genesis version the world has become so violent that God decides to start again, by destroying all creatures bar those saved by Noah, who is the one righteous man remaining. You know the story: God sends the flood and destroys all living things.

He blotted out every living thing that was on the face of the ground, human beings and animals and creeping things and birds of the air; they were blotted out from the earth. Only Noah was left, and those that were with him on the ark. (Genesis 7:23)

However, at the end of the flood God repents of this action and makes a commitment through a covenant with the whole of humanity never to destroy humanity again through natural disaster, signed by the gift of the rainbow.

God said, 'This is the sign of the covenant that I make between me and you and every living creature that is with you, for all future generations: I have set my bow in the clouds, and it shall be a sign of the covenant between me and the earth.' (Genesis 9:17)

There is also a tradition of interpretation of the Hebrew scriptures that warns us against too easily associating God's action with the forces of nature. In the story of Elijah in 1 Kings 18 and 19 – after playing with magic, claiming it's a demonstration of Yahweh's power, and therefore outwitting the prophets of Baal – Elijah, fearful of Jezebel's fury, retreats to the mountain and goes into hiding (so much for confidence in Yahweh!). But here Elijah learns that God is not in the natural forces of wind, thunder and earthquake, but is to be found in the still small voice of silence.

God's transcendence is affirmed not in demonstrations of power, but in the still small voice that comes in the silence – a most powerful stillness. God's Otherness as God's radical love, God's transcendence as the still small voice beyond the forces of nature – creating in love, letting go in love, redeeming in love, sending us the Spirit in love – a love so beyond our own understanding, so radical in its nature, that it is beyond our total comprehension – prefiguring, some Christian interpreters might say, the non-violent God revealed in Jesus Christ.

We need to hear the Qur'anic corrective of 'God is Great' to avoid us slipping into turning this wild love of God into a simplistic sweetener, to avoid turning Jesus into a saccharin saviour. But we need to offer in dialogue with our Muslim brothers and sisters in Abraham the revelation of God in Jesus Christ – in his life, death and resurrection, in his radical, outrageous love – and we need to do so through our prayers and our actions.

So whilst I give thanks for the Qur'anic corrective and challenge to our often sentimentalised version of the God of love, I also want to offer the understanding of God in Christianity; the inherent paradox at the heart of Christianity that needs to be held as a tension: God's sovereignty as Creator and vulnerability in the Incarnation of Christ, and additionally the promise of dwelling in the heart of believers and beyond through the Holy Spirit 'who blows where it wills'.

I want to tell my Muslim friends that I love the *islam* they have revealed to me: the beautiful path of finding peace in surrendering to God through disciplined practice, the fantastically liberating discipline of prayer brought into the everyday, a source for the constant reminder of who we are – creatures made to worship God – and a challenge to our naturally idolatrous ways.[2]

But I so much also want to share what might be called the *islam* of Christ – the one who in his very being showed how humanity and divinity embrace as one. You want to know God? – look at Jesus, *look* at him, this is how much God loves us: he is not only merciful, slow to anger, but willing to become vulnerable; promises not only to abstain from violence, as in the rainbow story in Genesis, but to receive human violence onto God's very self – to take it, absorb it and transform it through resurrection.

'The broken heart that lets the whole world fall in' – victims of the earthquake, jerry-building profiteers, calculating government officials, desperate people who walk over others to get to scarce supplies – his all-embracing love cannot but lead us to weep over our sins and failings and to submit to that love. To follow his *islam*, his submission, his path of peace, through the practice of forgiveness, mercy and compassion. To forgive as Jesus forgives, to be merciful as Jesus is merciful, and to love as Jesus loves. The *islam* of Christ is about making this so – becoming a merciful, compassionate and loving people.

And we become such people through prayer, through the constant prayer that we can learn from our Muslim neighbours, during times like Ramadan, to allow a God-consciousness to break into the everyday of our lives. A Muslim friend of mine says that it is only in prayer five times a day, as he prostrates himself, that he knows for sure that his heart is ruling his head.

We live in a beautiful but also chaotic world. At the heart of it all, faith tells us, is God: the God of love. The Hebrews and their neighbours the Canaanites saw the sea as a sign of chaos, and believed that Yahweh or Baal saved them from the chaos of the seas and other fearful forces of nature.

In Christian baptism we are submerged in the waters of chaos and are called to rise and love. The symbol of baptism is not so much about cleansing as overcoming chaos. John baptised to cleanse. Jesus calls us to baptism in order to overcome chaos, as he overcame the chaos of destruction and death in his crucifixion and resurrection. We are submerged in the waters of chaos, but rise and love, and in loving reveal that the world is won for God.

In a world of chaos, disaster and confusion we are called to become lovers, to proclaim the enthronement of love over chaos, however chaos manifests itself, in natural disaster or human oppression. That is why we are here, that is why we worship – to learn to love more.

That is why we are called to be Church, to become a school for love. So that in our worship, prayer and action we proclaim the truth of the God of love who creates, redeems and sustains us.

Footnotes

1. Some translate Allâhu Akbar! as God is greater!

2. I also love the fact that Muslims honour Jesus. One evening I was walking past the Makkah Masjid as my friend Assan and some of the younger activists at the mosque were putting finishing touches to a poster advertising an event to be addressed by the international Sufi teacher Hamza Yusef. My friends greeted me and said that they were thinking what a good idea it would be to have a permanent billboard outside the mosque saying 'We love Jesus': It was a humorous remark

offering a Muslim alternative to the traditional church wayside pulpit's 'Jesus Loves You'. But the truth is Muslims *do* love Jesus, and sometimes Christians find this threatening, as obviously Islam says some different things about the one whom we see as the central revelation of our faith; but this love of Jesus can be a point of dialogue and an opportunity to share.

Note: In their contributions to this book, I think that both Salma and Firdaws beautifully demonstrate how an Islamic understanding of God's transcendence and oneness can also lead to a spirituality of the practice of love. The intriguing point to be made is that the very different theologies and understandings of God's action and being can lead to the same practice: believers being inspired to live love.

Chapter seven

No god but God

It was a small gathering: only myself, Charles, the diocesan interfaith advisor, Zaheer and Qasim from the Grand Mosque, and a man I hadn't met before, pacing around on the other side of the room. The gathering was the Hyde Park leg of the 'Trust or Terror' meetings, organised by the diocesan interfaith advisor for the second Together for Peace festival in Leeds in autumn 2005. The poor attendance was not to do with the lack of interest in interfaith issues in the area but because only two weeks earlier we had had a hugely successful event in the same building, organised by a committee predominantly made up of women of faith, Muslim and Christian, led by Raihanna Ismail of the Multicultural Centre and local community activist Pat Regan. Several hundred Christians, Muslims, Hindus and those of no faith were in attendance, celebrating the diversity in faith and culture of our local community with, amongst other things, contemporary *nasheeds* and Christian hip-hop!

This was a very different kind of event.

Charles encouraged everyone to tuck into the assorted delicious food spread out on the table. I was chatting to Qasim and enjoying my second samosa, when I heard the large man who had been pacing about on the other side of the room say, in a loud voice: 'I'll consider apologising for the Crusades when Muslims apologise for their aggressive conquest of Christian lands long before the Crusades.' The man's remark was in reaction to an event that was going to take place the next day at the Grand Mosque after *jummah* prayers, as part of the Together for Peace festival. Representatives of the Christian Reconcilia-

tion Walk were going to address Muslims in the Grand
Mosque about their project and why they had wanted to
perform what they saw as an act of atonement for the violence
of the Crusades. The man found this distasteful and was
telling Zaheer, who at that time was Chair of the Grand
Mosque, in no uncertain terms, why. Zaheer's attempt to
placate him with a 'Well, many bad things have been done in
the name of our religions but at heart we worship the same
God' was like showing a red rag to a bull, as the man spluttered
over his food and stabbed his finger in Zaheer's direction,
saying: 'The God of the Bible is not the same as Allah as far as
I'm concerned! What our Lord Jesus Christ teaches us is
completely opposite to what the Qur'an teaches!' I think it was
Charles who diplomatically intervened and brought the
confrontation to an end. Soon afterwards, the man left.

I later learnt from one of our café volunteers, who attends
the same church as this brother, that he is involved with an
organisation that works to help persecuted Christians in
Muslims lands. He had obviously come to the meeting to make
his point and leave. Someone involved in the lives of Christians who face persecution in some Muslim-majority countries
for just practising their Christianity must see such events as a
kind of betrayal, and people like myself, engaged in deep
dialogue and encounter, as traitors to the faith. But I came
away from that evening with a feeling of sadness over the fact
that in his aggression and confrontation he had not demonstrated anything of the way of Christ he sought to proclaim.
How had he shared Christ's love for Muslims with Zaheer?
And was getting into a conflict about who has persecuted
whom the worst living up to what Jesus demands of the costly
way of love, including praying for persecutors? Surely, I

thought, as I sat in the Grand Mosque the day after – with over 200 of the congregation staying behind after prayers to listen to Lynn Green from the Reconciliation Walk gently share his understanding of what they had done and why – *this* evangelical initiative was much more powerfully sharing Christ, whilst also challenging easy Muslim stereotypes of Christians.

Lynn read out the original founding statement of the Reconciliation Walk to the gathered Muslims:

'*Nine hundred years ago, our forefathers carried the name of Jesus Christ in battle across the Middle East. Fuelled by fear, greed and hatred, they betrayed the name of Christ by conducting themselves in a manner contrary to His wishes and character. The Crusaders lifted the banner of the Cross above your people. By this act, they corrupted its true meaning of reconciliation, forgiveness and selfless love.*

On the anniversary of the First Crusade, we also carry the name of Christ. We wish to retrace the footsteps of the Crusaders in apology for their deeds and in demonstration of the true meaning of the Cross. We deeply regret the atrocities committed in the name of Christ by our predecessors. We renounce greed, hatred and fear, and condemn all violence done in the name of Jesus Christ.

Where they were motivated by hatred and prejudice, we offer love and brotherhood. Jesus the Messiah came to give life. Forgive us for allowing His name to be associated with death. Please accept again the true meaning of the Messiah's words: 'The Spirit of the Lord is upon me, because He has anointed me to bring good news to the poor. He has sent me to proclaim release to the captives and recovery of sight to the blind, to let the oppressed go free, to proclaim the year of the Lord's favour.'

As we go, we bless you in the name of the Lord Jesus Christ.'

We can get a flavour of what the Reconciliation Walk felt the need to repent of, from an eyewitness report of the taking of Jerusalem by Crusaders on 15 July, 1099:

One of our men by the name of Laethold climbed on to the city wall. As soon as he succeeded, all the defenders took flight. Our people pursued them along the wall and through the city and killed and mutilated them. Then they went to the Temple of Solomon; there was such a fight that we were up to our knees in the blood of our enemies ... Soon our people ran through the city and took booty of gold, silver, horses, mules, plundering houses full of goods. Then they all assembled, full of enthusiasm and weeping for joy, at the tomb of our saviour Jesus; they worshipped and dedicated their lives to him. The next morning they quietly went on the roof of the temple, seized men and women of the Saracens and cut off their heads with the naked sword.[1]

With such stories in our past, is it any wonder that the history and current reality of Muslim-Christian relations is an uneasy one? The man at the diocesan event and our friends at the Reconciliation Walk represent two different approaches, both coming out of the modern Evangelical tradition of the church, to the history and current reality of Muslim-Christian relations. It is the demonstration to me of the difference between an approach based on confrontation and one built on developing relationship, one based on aggressive proselytising and one rooted in a gentle and humble loving witness.

But what of those early conquests by Muslims referred to by our concerned brother? How did Christians in the overtaken

areas respond? In the early Muslim conquests of the area we
know as the Middle East, the relationship of some Christians
to Islam, and indeed Islam to Christianity, was not as hostile or
as antagonistic as our friend claims. If we examine the time of
the Prophet Muhammad himself, Islamic sources tell us of an
interesting encounter at Medina when some Byzantine Christians from the Yemen came to debate the nature of Christ with
Muhammad. When they asked Muhammad where in the city
they might go to pray, he told them to use the mosque. Reza
Shah Kezemi has argued that the Yemeni Christians actually
performed a Eucharist in the mosque at Medina, with the
Prophet's blessing.[2] And in a letter to the monks of Saint
Catherine at Mount Sinai, Muhammad said:

> This is a message from Muhammad ibn Abdullah, as a
> covenant to those who adopt Christianity, near and far, we are
> with them. Verily I, the servants, the helpers, and my followers
> defend them, because Christians are my citizens; and by Allah!
> I hold out against anything that displeases them. No compul-
> sion is to be on them. Neither are their judges to be removed
> from their jobs nor their monks from their monasteries. No one
> is to destroy a house of their religion, to damage it, or to carry
> anything from it to the Muslims' houses. Should anyone take
> any of these, he would spoil God's covenant and disobey his
> Prophet. Verily, they are my allies and have my secure charter
> against all that they hate. No one is to force them to travel or
> to oblige them to fight. The Muslims are to fight for them. If a
> female Christian is married to a Muslim, it is not to take place
> without her approval. She is not to be prevented from visiting
> her church to pray. Their churches are to be respected. They are
> neither to be prevented from repairing them nor the sacredness

*of their covenants. No one of the nation (Muslims) is to
disobey the covenant till the Last Day (end of the world).*[3]

It is important to remember that evidence for this period is
scant and ideas of what was actually going on are debated
amongst scholars. But the Jesuit Ovey Mohammed, drawing
upon that scholarship, has put forward the possible scenario
that, for some Christians in the Middle East, the early
conquests of Islam spelt liberation from an oppressive Byzantine Empire.[4] Islam represented for many an indigenous revolt
against the imperialism that had in various guises dominated
the area and subverted indigenous languages and traditions
since Alexander the Great's conquest in 324 BCE. Indeed,
Christianity itself, when it became the religion of the empire
under Constantine, became part of this cultural imperialism,
as a tight unity in doctrine became seen as a necessity for the
empire's political stability. The orthodox debates about the
nature of Christ and the Trinity in the early Church councils,
culminating at the Council of Chalcedon in 451, were to the
detriment of the expressions of Middle Eastern churches. An
alliance between the Greek-speaking and Latin-speaking
churches sought to force an orthodoxy onto these churches,
whose first language was neither Greek nor Latin but Syriac,
Armenian or Coptic. The Greek- and Latin-speaking churches
had a privileged position in the linguistic minefield of the
debates on the nature of Christ and the Trinity, as Latin and
Greek was the theological language of the councils. Ovey
Mohammed sees this as an issue of inculturation. The Middle
Eastern churches split off, and faced persecution under Byzantine authority for being heretical for over 200 years.[5] This led
to a rejection of official imperial orthodox Christianity. This

was the context in which Islam expanded in the Middle East, including the taking of Jerusalem at the time of the *Rashidun*, 'The Four Rightly Guided Caliphs', of Sunni Islam.

I do not want to romanticise the early spread of Islam. There were clear examples of incidents of persecution, including the attempted forced conversion (counter to Qur'anic principle) and then massacre of the Byzantine garrison at Gaza. But I do want to challenge a simplistic picture, as perpetuated by many Christians today, of a victimisation of a pure Christianity in these early conquests. The story is indeed more complex. It is worth noting that for over 300 years after the initial conquest of Jerusalem by Islam, Christians, Muslims and Jews lived there in harmony, until restrictions on pilgrims and harassment of Christians began in the tenth century with the Fatmid caliphs. It then somewhat intensified when the Turkish Seljuks took possession of the Holy Land, although reports from returning pilgrims that formed one of the catalysts for the Crusades are thought to have exaggerated the extent of the oppression. It is worth quoting Hugh Goddard in the conclusion of his assessment of Muslim rule up to the end of the medieval period:

> *By medieval standards, the Muslim treatment of Jews and Christians was relatively tolerant and liberal, though it was clearly, by modern standards, still discriminatory to some extent. Comparisons can only fairly be made with other medieval societies, and on this basis the Muslim world scores extremely well.*[6]

The context of the division in the Middle East, between Byzantine and local expressions of Christianity, meant that the first theological interpretations of Islam by Christians were not negative.[7] The non-Chalcedonian churches initially drew on the Book of Genesis and the story of Hagar and Ishmael to explain the rise of Islam, seeing it as the fulfilment of the promises made to Hagar about the descendants of Ishmael. Twice God makes the promise, first to Abraham and then to Hagar, that he will make a great nation of Ishmael. An Armenian bishop in the seventh century said of Muhammad: 'He taught them (the Arabs) to know the God of Abraham.' Secondly, non-Chalcedonian churches saw Islam as a judgement from God on a corrupt Byzantine Christianity. A Christian-Syrian writer of the 12th century, looking back, stated:

> *The God of vengeance ... raised up from the south the children of Ishmael to deliver us from the hands of the Romans ... it was no light benefit for us to be freed from the cruelty of the Romans, their wickedness, anger and ardent cruelty towards us, and to find ourselves in peace.*[8]

It is interesting that these two initial theological responses saw God positively involved in the development of Islam. It wasn't until those who had pledged loyalty to the Byzantine Church, but remained in conquered lands, began to respond, that theological reflection on Islam became more negative. This was most clearly represented in the work of John of Damascus, who was a senior civil servant in an Islamic administration before becoming a monk and priest. He argued that Islam was a form of Christian heresy. It is this response that formed the basis of much Christian apologetics in response to Islam down the proceeding centuries.

I want to suggest a return to those two initial theological

responses to Islam in our context today. On the one hand we face the challenge of the biblical texts on the promises God made to Ishmael; and on the other we can explore how encountering Islam, as a faith that as well as sharing roots often conflicts with the Christian gospel, might help to shine the light of God's judgement upon us as Christians. It might clarify, for example, the ways we have failed, through triumphalism and power-seeking, to share the truth about Jesus the saviour who reveals the non-violent path of the revolutionary Kingdom of God: the Jesus of Shalom, or even *Salaam.*

Karl Josef Kuschel says:

> *There can really be no doubt that the Hebrew Bible made significant statements about Ishmael – not only biographical but also theological ... these statements urgently need evaluation. For Ishmael is the forefather of the Arabian tribes and thus of Islam. To continue to ignore this aspect theologically would be an indication of a pernicious blindness to God ... God evidently has special plans for Ishmael, which can only be ignored by those trapped in a salvation-historical arrogance.*[9]

He then goes on to outline five aspects of the story in Genesis that require that we recognise Ishmael's special status.

Firstly, although Genesis is concerned primarily with the story of Isaac, Ishmael *is* Abraham's first-born; also, the literal meaning of Ishmael's name is 'God hears'. It is this first-born status that has such symbolic power for Muslims. Secondly, Ishmael receives the sign of God's covenant, circumcision, at the same time as Abraham, before Isaac is even born. Ishmael is therefore accepted into God's covenant. Such a reading undermines any attempt by Judaism to absolutise its own election. Thirdly, not only Isaac's life but also Ishmael's stands under God's protection. Ishmael's life is twice saved by God's intervention. In the first story, Hagar is driven into the wilderness by Sarah's cruelty, but God sends an angel who comforts her with the news that 'I will make your descendants so numerous that they cannot be counted.' Some have argued that this passage does not contain a blessing but a curse, as the angel says:

Now you have conceived and shall bear a son;
you shall call him Ishmael,
for the Lord has given heed to your affliction.
He shall be a wild ass of a man,
with his hand against everyone,
and everyone's hand against him;
and he shall live at odds with all his kin.

Gen 16:11b–12

However, Jonathan Culver has argued:

Genesis 16:12 is given in the context of a promise to Hagar. It would be strange indeed for the covenant angel to try and motivate Hagar to return to Abraham's tent by pronouncing a curse on her child! Accordingly, the wild donkey metaphor is better understood in light of passages like Job 39:5–8. Here God describes the wild donkey as a freedom-loving creature and a wilderness wanderer. This is an apt image of what Ishmael and his descendants were later to become – Bedouin nomads, free from the yoke of domination. This would have been good news for Hagar, a slave woman, as she trembled at the thought of facing Sara's wrath.[10]

141

The second story is more confusing, for God both agrees to Hagar and Ishmael's expulsion yet also saves them. We are told that 'God was with the lad, and he grew up; he lived in the wilderness and became an expert with the bow.' Clearly here in Jewish scripture we are told that God's covenant with Isaac cannot be absolutised, for, as Kuschel's fourth point makes clear, Ishmael stands under God's blessing too and his people will have a significant future:

> 'As for Ishmael, I have heard you; I will bless him and make him fruitful and exceedingly numerous; he shall be the father of twelve princes, and I will make him a great nation.'
> (Genesis 17:20)

Finally, it is significant that not only Isaac but Ishmael is at Abraham's burial, reappearing in the narrative despite us having heard nothing about him since his expulsion. He holds a unique position: he is neither like Isaac nor like Abraham's other children by his second wife, Keturah. Something special is going on for him. God has plans … plans that the descendants of Isaac, in the guise of Judaism and Christianity, have always found problematic and confusing. We, like Sarah, have often sought to banish Ishmael into the wilderness. Interpreting this story in this way calls us, in our time, to a serious Abrahamic dialogue, not denying our differences but perhaps being willing to acknowledge that the confusing Abrahamic dynamic represented in the religious traditions of Judaism, Christianity and Islam may in some sense be God-given. It is only through opening our hearts and minds to one another, whilst also communicating with enthusiasm and courage what we feel has been revealed to us in our traditions, that God's truth for us all will be more fully revealed.

In developing a contemporary version of the second response of the non-Chalcedonian churches to the rise of Islam, we might begin to question the role of empire in Christian history, from the beginning of Rome's embrace of Christianity, through the Byzantine Empire, the rise of Western Christianity and the Crusades and Western imperialism; and how, as the Reconciliation Walk clearly pointed out, these Christian accommodations to power and authority have diluted and destroyed the proclamation of the non-violent, self-giving God revealed in Jesus Christ. Might we be able to acknowledge that in some sense Islam, in its powerful 'No' to our Christological and Trinitarian formulations, could be God's judgement on Chalcedonian Christianity's roots, in accommodation to the political requirements of empire rather than being genuine theological exploration? Might we also hear it as a judgement on the accommodation to empire and political power that has been made down the ages in the Crusades and Western imperialism? I am not calling for a Christian acceptance of Qur'anic critique of Christology and the doctrine of the Trinity, or saying that Islam exclusively be defined as arising only in order to get Christians back on the right path. What I am saying is that we can allow the Qur'anic critique to speak to us in such a way that it becomes a corrective to our triumphalist distortions of the creating, redeeming, empowering, self-giving God revealed in the Christian story. In this way it can assist us in representing the God of love revealed in Jesus Christ, as we seek to walk boldly in his way, following his path of self-giving love in our relationship with Islam. We have to acknowledge that many Muslims throughout the world think the US empire is a Christian empire: George Bush all but announced the war on Afghanistan from the pulpit of the National Cathedral in

Washington DC in 2001; after dropping the language of Crusade for the 'War on Terror', the invasion of Afghanistan was labelled 'infinite justice'. Vice President Dick Cheney sent the following greetings on his Christmas card in 2003: *And if a sparrow cannot fall to the ground without His notice, is it probable that an empire can rise without His aid?* The idols of empire, nationalism and patriotism are dressed up in the symbols and language of Christianity, often with figures like Billy Graham in support. Our response to this should be to find models from the history of Muslim-Christian encounter that witness to a truer representation of Christianity to our Muslim brothers and sisters.

One such example is St Francis at the time of the Crusades. When Pope Innocent III launched his campaign for a Fifth Crusade in 1213, in order to recapture Jerusalem from the control of Islam, the whole of the Christian Church in Europe was recruited to the cause and it became a central feature of Church life. Crusade preachers were commissioned, special prayers added to the liturgy and sacrificial financial giving encouraged. The Crusades were organised under the slogan *'Dues vult'*, 'God wills it', and St Bernard was not unusual in his attitude that 'to kill a Muslim is not murder'. After Innocent died in 1216, whilst touring to drum up support for the Crusade, Pope Honorius III replaced him and on his inauguration issued a fresh call for the whole of Christendom to become involved in raising money and in praying for a new Crusade. He added a large degree of moral pressure when he wrote that those who did not put their names to a Crusade were guilty of 'the vice of ingratitude and the crime of infidelity'. However, Francis appears not to have reflected upon this decree, or upon any decrees making reference to the

Crusades, although he wrote to his brothers in the Franciscan order about most papal documents of the time, including significant decrees on the Eucharist and penance. Neither is there any record of the Franciscans participating in this campaign in any way, including the call for special prayers and acts of penance to receive God's blessing on the endeavour. Franciscan historians have reflected upon this, and concluded that St Francis and the brothers chose to resist the call to Crusade by non-compliance with the campaign, which they saw as a denial of, rather than a witness to, the gospel.[11]

Francis went even further when the Crusade was actually launched – he sought to persuade the Pope to have a change of heart. When that failed, he travelled to Egypt himself, to where the Crusaders were laying siege to the city of Damietta, and attempted to persuade the Christian Commander Cardinal Pelagius to end the fighting. When he refused, Francis crossed over to the other side and sought an audience with the Muslim leader, Sultan Malik al-Kamil. He wanted to let the Sultan know that the Crusaders did not represent, in their violence and warmongering, the true spirit of Jesus Christ. He wanted to give witness to God's love in Jesus Christ. In his biography of St Francis, St Bonaventure wrote of the event:

> *The sultan asked them by whom and why and in what capacity they had been sent, and how they got there; but Francis replied intrepidly that they had been sent by God, not by man, to show him and his subjects the way of salvation and proclaim the truth of the gospel message.*
>
> *When the sultan saw his enthusiasm and courage, he listened to him willingly and pressed him to stay with him ... then he offered Francis a number of valuable presents, but the saint*

> *was anxious only for the salvation of souls, he had no interest*
> *in the things of the earth and so he scorned them all as if they*
> *were so much dust. The sultan was lost in admiration at the*
> *sight of such perfect disregard for worldly wealth and he felt*
> *greater respect than ever for the saint.*[12]

Francis went to Egypt longing to bring the Crusaders to repentance and, through his peaceful and risky witness, the Muslims to a Christian belief in Jesus as Saviour. He seems to have failed on both accounts. But if he held on to the powerful sense of being sent by God, did he come to an understanding that it was *he* who was converted to a deeper understanding of God in the process? Arising out of a living, loving witness comes an openness to the Muslim faith and Islam as a spiritual path, and an ability to learn and grow in understanding of God through the process of encounter and witness.

Some contemporary commentators have argued that during his time in the Middle East, Francis was affected by what he saw of the practice of Islam.[13] Sometime after Francis returned to Italy, he wrote his 'Letter to the Rulers of the People' in which he instructs them, maybe having been influenced by the *Adhan*, the Call to Prayer: 'See to it that God is held in great reverence among your subjects; every evening, at a signal given by a herald or in some other way, praise and thanks should be given to the Lord God Almighty by all the people.' He was also apparently influenced by the practice of prostration in Muslim prayers. In his 'Letter to a General Chapter of the Franciscans', he writes: 'At the sound of God's name you should fall to the ground and adore him with fear and reverence.' The reason friars are sent all over the world, he adds, is to 'bear witness … that there is no other Almighty God besides him', echoing the Muslim *Shahada*: 'There is no god but God!'

Some have argued that some of Francis's later prayers were influenced by his contact with the Muslim practice of reciting the ninety-nine names of God, including The Gracious, The Kindly, The Beneficent, The High One, The Merciful, The Compassionate, The Mighty, The Loving ... Francis's prayer 'The Praises of God' could well have been influenced by this aspect of Islamic spirituality:

You are holy, Lord, the only God, and Your deeds are wonderful.

You are strong.
You are great.
You are the Most High.
You are Almighty.
You, Holy Father, are King of heaven and earth.

You are Three and One,
Lord God, all Good,
You are Good, all Good, supreme Good,
Lord God, living and true.

You are love.
You are wisdom.
You are humility.
You are endurance.
You are rest.
You are peace.
You are joy and gladness.
You are justice and moderation.
You are all our riches.
And You suffice for us.

You are beauty.
You are gentleness.
You are our protector.
You are our guardian and defender.
You are courage.
You are our haven and our hope.

You are our faith,
our great consolation.
You are our eternal life,
Great and Wonderful Lord,
God Almighty,
Merciful Saviour.
Amen [14]

Did this seeming influence of Islamic spirituality upon his own prayer life signify a greater appreciation for the presence of God in Islam? In his last draft of the rule of the Order, Francis encourages that brothers be allowed to minister amongst Muslims. He prioritises a mission and witness of loving action over direct proselytisation, insisting they avoid quarrels and disputation with Muslims and work at acts of service and love relating to all human beings. Only after doing this, 'if it pleases God', are they to preach the faith in words.

The liberation theologian and Franciscan Leonardo Boff sees in the story of Francis at Damietta, the saint offering a model for dialogue with Islam:

1. *We must seize the initiative; we should not wait for the other to come to us.*

2. *We must trust others because they are our brothers and sisters.*

3. We must live, work and insert ourselves in the other's world.

4. We must place ourselves in minor and servile positions, and we must renounce pretension that we are superior or privileged because we are Christians.

5. We must realise that it is better to understand than to be understood, it is better to love than to be loved, and we must also make ourselves an instrument of peace.

6. We must put everything in the context of prayer and spirituality.

7. We must always connect human peace with God's peace so that peace is long-lasting and complete.[15]

Alongside this practical relational loving witness is the need to recover the radical anti-imperialism of Jesus and the early Church. The 'one and only Saviour' language of the New Testament, which is so often used by conservative evangelicals to dismiss engagement with other faith traditions, is, I would maintain, better interpreted as a resistance to empire. The early Church grew up in the shadow of the Roman Empire with its claims to power and the claims of emperors of being divine: the language of the New Testament in its supposed exclusivism is addressing the context of idolatrous worship of the false gods of empire and wealth. The early Christians developed counter-cultural communities that challenged the Roman and Greek worlds' structured and fixed hierarchies. The earliest creed, 'Jesus is Lord', was in direct rebellion to the claims of the divinity of the emperor. The radical gospel that Paul proclaimed that said there was neither Jew nor Greek, male nor female, slave nor free, for 'all are one in Christ Jesus', was in direct contrast to and excluded the hierarchies of the

Greek and Roman political and familial structures. These exclusive claims of the gospel are relevant to us today when we are seduced by the pull of counter-allegiances, be that to government, a political party, to the ideologies of nationalism and patriotism, capitalism and militarism.

The great religions of the world are allies in this struggle, this jihad; most importantly when they help us in their critique to identify this accommodation.

An openness to other genuine paths is rooted in the early Church. Not denying its Jewish roots, the early Church sought to expand the vision of covenant in Judaism into the Gentile world, drawing upon the inclusive vision of the radical prophets. The strong argumentative language of the New Testament in relation to Judaism is part of a family argument, and it is also part of a larger process of change that was going on in Judaism at the time. Christianity was a movement that came from Judaism and continues to share a hopeful vision of the future coming of God's Kingdom of Shalom. Other movements transformed Judaism from what it was in Jesus and Paul's time to what it became through the development of Rabbinical Judaism after the destruction of the temple in AD 70. Christianity was less a superseding of Judaism and more of a development (as Paul shows in Romans 9–11) of the Jewish story into the Gentile world, with a radical new twist – the resurrection had begun. The development and strengthening of Rabbinical Judaism renewed the tradition of the Mosaic covenant, and so the older tradition of Sinai continued alongside the new tradition of Easter, both speaking and living God's story, to be joined six centuries later in the Abrahamic dynamic by the descendants of Ishmael in their response to the Qur'an's imperative.

The first Christian theologians included in their variety a strong inclusive strand. Justin Martyr believed that 'seeds' of the Word of God had been scattered throughout the intellectual traditions of the world. Origen was by no means alone in his radically universalist vision of seeing all as being saved within the Love of God; and Clement of Alexandria saw saving efficacy not only in Greek philosophy but in Hinduism and Buddhism!

This threefold model of practical and loving witness to the truth of Christ – resistance and repudiation of empire and openness to the truth present in the other – is how we can engage with Islam. This is a call to live Christ in our very being in relation to Muslims, and it is a call and a challenge that is relevant for today. This is not naivety that is unwilling in some politically correct fashion to critique Islam – but a following of the commands of Jesus. Until we have removed the log from our own eye we will be unable to address the splinter in our brother's. We need to become in our faith in Jesus Christ, people who respond to his call: 'Come, follow me.' We should become a living Christological statement – our creed becomes our embodiment of Christ in the here and now, in how we relate to Muslims, as Francis learned and practised at the time of the Fifth Crusade. In our current context of the 'War on Terror', Islamophobia and the culture of fear perpetuated by an empire which in its public statements often recruits the language of Christian faith to its cause, we need Christians living alongside Muslims to show an alternative. We need to be people of the way of forgiveness, reconciliation and self-giving love, resisting empire not with an agenda of the conversion of the other in order to build the church to rule the world, but with the vision of discipleship given to us in the parables of Jesus. In the leaven in the dough and the salt flavouring the food, we have images of the Kingdom that call for a practice that seeks not to dominate and control but to contribute unique and essential ingredients to a wholesome vision, responding with resurrection faith to the prophetic demand: to live justly, love mercy and walk humbly with our God.

Footnotes

1. Quoted in *Christianity without Absolutes*, Reinhold Bernhardt, SCM Press, 1994

2. Reza Shah Kezemi, 'Defining Without Confining: Reflections on a Prophetic Usage of Sacred Space', *Interreligious Insight*, July, 2005

3. Letter to the monks of Saint Catherine at Mount Sinai – from http://www.aph.gov.au/library/pubs/cib/2001-02/02cib07.htm

4. Ovey N. Mohammed, S.J., *Muslim-Christian Relations – Past, Present, Future*, Orbis Books, 1999

5. Modern ecumenical developments have led to an increasing acceptance that many of the minority non-Chalcedonian churches are not heretical at all. The churches, which now come under the umbrella of 'Oriental Orthodoxy', have been involved in positive relations with the primary Eastern Orthodox, Roman Catholic, Anglican and ecumenical Protestant authorities.

6. Hugh Goddard, *A History of Christian-Muslim Relations*, Edinburgh University Press, 2000

7. See Hugh Goddard, *A History of Christian-Muslim Relations*, Edinburgh University Press, 2000, from which most of the information in the following paragraphs is drawn.

8. Quoted in Hugh Goddard, *A History of Christian-Muslim Relations*, Edinburgh University Press, 2000

9. Karl Josef Kuschel, *Abraham: A Sign of Hope for Jews, Christians and Muslims*, SCM Press, 1995, p.131–2

10. Jonathan Culver, 'The Ishmael Promise and Contextualisation Among Muslims', *International Journal of Frontier Mission*, Volume 17:1, Spring 2000

11. See *Francis and Islam* by J. Hoeberichts, Franciscan Press, 1997

12. Quoted in *Saint Francis and the Foolishness of God*, Marie Dennis, Joseph Narshe, OFM, Cynthia Moe-Lobeda, Stuart Taylor, Orbis Books, 13th edition © 1993, p.85

13. See Leonhard Lehmann, 'Francis's Two Letters to the Custodes: Proposals for Christian-Islamic Ecumenism in Praising God' in *Greyfriars Review 2*, December 1988, p.63–91

14. 'The Praises of God', St Francis – from the National Shrine of Saint Francis website: www.shrinesf.org/prayers.htm#pb

15. Leonardo Boff, from *Fundamentalism, Terrorism and the Future of Humanity*, Leonardo Boff, SPCK, 2006, p.56–57

Dialogue

Chapter eight

Sisterly solidarity

Annie Heppenstall

Ray first came to my attention in 2002 when I read a newspaper article about a priest arrested for demonstrating his opposition to the invasion of Afghanistan by sitting down in the middle of one of the main roads in Leeds. There was a photo of someone who could have been mistaken for a biker staring defiantly at the camera, and an affirmation of support from his bishop. At the time I was off work long-term sick and not up to engaging with the outside world as such, but this article woke me up. 'Good for him,' I remember thinking, 'where were all the rest of the priests?' In the instant, I decided that as a Christian I could not agree with military aggression either, then consigned the paper to the recycling bin.

Some two years later, much recovered, I visited All Hallows Church for the first time, not because I wanted to meet the priestly road-blocker, but because Kathy Galloway, Leader of the Iona Community, was visiting and I wanted to hear her speak. In fact, I had forgotten about the newspaper article, and did not make a connection until later with this and the announcement that the Vicar, Ray, was delayed at the Iraqi border, hence his absence from church. Looking back, it is amazing how little that meant to me at the time: Ray's whole approach to his journey in Iraq and Syria is surely unique in contemporary Christian engagement with Islam – disarmingly and alarmingly vulnerable. I find his account wildly challenging to the church as an institution – the thought of a priest just wandering the streets of war-torn Karbala during Ashura, eating and sleeping among the people wherever he was offered hospitality. I didn't know he was there when I saw it, but I remember watching the news of the horrific bomb blast which happened streets away from where he was. The trust – faith – he demonstrated putting his life in the hands of his Muslim hosts and of God is an immense gesture in interfaith bridge-building.

After my initial visit I decided All Hallows to be a good church to bring my son to, and some time later asked Ray about developing my engagement with Islam. I'm not sure quite what I expected, perhaps that he would give me a book to read or introduce me to a friendly family nearby, but having explained some of my background he agreed to take me to visit a local Shi'a mosque. What this involved demonstrated to a T Ray's in-at-the-deep-end teaching style! We walked unceremoniously through the main entrance together, and placed our shoes in pigeonholes. Ray then promptly disappeared through a door on the right, greeted enthusiastically as he went by a gathering of young men hanging around the door, while I found myself gently but firmly ushered through a door on the left, into a room filled entirely with mainly black-clad women and children. There I stayed for the next two and a half hours, on a fast learning curve! I will come back to this experience later, but I mention it here because it illustrates my feeling that a female Christian encounter with Islam is likely to be quite different to a male Christian (especially a male priest) encounter with Islam. There are points of contact between Ray's experience and my own much less dramatic encounter with Islam, because for part of the time we were both involved in the same events, same city, same church, same parish, same issues. But the difference I found often stemmed from the common Muslim pattern of two worlds: a world of men and a world of women.

My interest in Islam was awakened when I was at university, doing a degree in Theology and Religious Studies. I studied aspects of Christianity, Hinduism, Buddhism and Judaism, but was disappointed to find that Islamic Studies was not available; naturally, this became the subject I hankered to learn about. I graduated knowing my education was incomplete, a feeling that haunted me when I took up my first post as a primary school teacher in an inner-city school where a large percentage of the children were Muslim. I spent eight years there and got to know whole families quite well, although most of my experience of Islam was through the children and their mothers. While the families were extremely likeable almost without exception, occasionally I had concerns about what I saw and heard, mainly from a feminist perspective. This included accounts of heavy-handed males in the home and at the mosque schools, subordinate women who 'lived' in the kitchen, pressure on very young children to fast, and on girls to take up extreme forms of veiling and enter into arranged marriages. I am aware that not following up my perceptions led me to an incomplete and uninformed picture of the whole, which I later came to feel I should address.

It was this concern which I described to Ray, as a relatively new member of his congregation seeking to restore my contact with Islam and learn more. And so it was that I found myself on the left-hand-side of a thick black curtain dividing the prayer room and screening men from women, in a Shi'a mosque during Ramadan. I had gone to some trouble to dress sensitively, wearing a long skirt, loose top and a scarf over my head. I did not look particularly out of place, which did not entirely help; seized with shyness, I stood looking around, until an older woman came up and welcomed me. 'I'm just visiting,' I began, 'I'm not really sure what to do, I've never been here before ...' 'Oh, it's all right,' she replied, 'it will be the same as the mosque where you normally go!' Having made such an effort to look like a Muslim, I balked at the fact that I now needed to declare myself a Christian; I was afraid this might not go down very well. But no matter, I was soon swept along to stand alongside the other women as lines began to form from the hubbub of talking friends, at the call of a male voice from the other side of the curtain. The lines of women all began to move in unison, arms, heads, prostrations in harmony with one another, not rigidly but with space for individuals to take their own time and still be together, like a sea of corn waving as the wind blows over it. My new friend nudged me: *This is what you do when you pray*, she was meaning, and I realised that I had the split-second choice to decline and go and sit at the back to watch, or join in. Some people might say I shouldn't have been so easily led, I should have checked what the words of the prayers meant first, and asked my vicar whether he thought it was appropriate or not. But he hadn't said a word about 'should and shouldn't', and anyway, he was on the other side of the black curtain, in another world. To me, this was a prayerful moment: the Arabic was clearly a song of awe and devotion towards God, mournful and joyful at the same time. The actions were an expression of humility and the lines a sign of equality among sisters who prayed with eyes closed in concentration, faces etched with sincerity. The question was not 'Should I or shouldn't I?' But *Do I want to be in this moment or outside it?* And then the next questions, following rapidly, were *Do I trust what is going on here, or not? Is God here, or not?* Well, God is ever-present, all-hearing and all-knowing and I wanted to step into the presence of God as these people were doing: like a new dish, how would I ever know what Muslim prayer was about unless I tried it for myself? So I joined in. Four years later at the time of writing, sometimes I still join in, and sometimes I don't, it depends how I and the situation feels.

The most powerful 'joining in' I have ever experienced, other than my first visit to the Shi'a mosque, was as a visitor to Dawn Prayer at a large mosque in Istanbul, where we stood on mats spread out over the pavement, thousands of men ahead of us. Shabby street vendors stood side by side with smartly dressed office workers, and I in my blue hijab stood as one of them, feeling not a sense of uncertainty about bowing to 'their' God, but a huge sense of awesome togetherness that transcended the barriers words create, and united in the spiritual longing hearts and souls share in their yearning for God. I was travelling at this time with a group made up of people of different faiths, including Ray. I believe it was a journey that made more impact on me than on Ray, he having had the extraordinarily deep experience of Iraq a couple of years earlier. Travelling together is a way of forging relationships – I know that Ray and his companion Hussein formed a strong friendship through their shared and very exceptional experiences. Although a humble and very 'safe' expedition in comparison, I naturally spent much of my time on this journey with Aazuman, the only other woman in the party. Aazuman is Turkish, and she and her husband jointly organised the journey. She did a great deal, simply by being herself, to challenge my earlier impression of what it is to be a Muslim woman, being highly committed to and articulate about her faith, a working mother with boundless energy, well-read, and enjoying a wonderfully warm, caring and humour-filled relationship with her husband. During this visit I was welcomed with open arms and a kiss on both cheeks by many women, and found that the common bond that overrode our faith differences was simply being a woman, and particularly, a mother: there is so much to talk about! It is so obvious it hardly needs saying, yet the truth that dawned on me was of common humanity, shared sisterhood. The warmth that came naturally from that connection seemed to mean that differences were not so much overlooked, but certainly respected and if not always fully understood, graciously accepted with the genuine generosity of a sincere host or hostess. This sense of receiving hospitality, of being the guest in another's territory, is something I have experienced frequently since, and reflect on as a way of considering my own role as a Christian 'visitor', in contrast to 'outside observer', keen to reciprocate warmth and appreciation at all times, and certainly before any serious discussion ensues. I find this reflected in the advice St Francis gives in the 13th century CE, that Christians should go humbly amongst the 'Saracens' and avoid arguments, although they should continue to confess Christ.

Back to my first visit to the Shi'a mosque: I expected, after prayers, for somebody to take the curtain across the room down because there was food to share. But no; huge white sheets were rolled out onto the floor and the women and children (who were free to wander between the two sides of the curtain) started to sit around the edges, helping to distribute bowls, soft drinks and cutlery. Several people had come to talk to me now, and I was warmly welcomed to come and sit with them; motherly fuss was made of me as I self-consciously excused myself as vegetarian, and a tray of plain rice and daal was produced. 'Do we not sit with the men?' I asked, worried that we were being shunned because 'they' didn't want to acknowledge our existence, and wondering how I was going to communicate with Ray when one or the other of us wanted to leave. 'Oh no, we like it better like this,' someone replied, 'we see enough of them at home! Now we're with our friends, we're all sisters!'

This 'them and us' division of the sexes is something I have met repeatedly since this first encounter, and is something I wrestle with. There seems to me, on the one hand, to be the capacity for a rich and deep bond among Muslim women – as I felt in my welcome by Turkish women – that I for one have not experienced very often among other groups of women I know, and which is very loving, very supportive and very attractive; I believe men form similarly close bonds. There have been times however, I have to say, when Ray has talked about plans to visit somewhere – the recitation at a mosque in Bradford which he describes in Chapter one, for example – when there appears not to have been a room or provision made for women, so that an experience such as this, which I would have been interested to attend, I could not have experienced, and certainly could not have shared with him, had I been able to attend, because it would have been amongst other women. The segregation of sexes continues to challenge me greatly, and I believe it is an issue which also challenges many contemporary Muslims and is affected by cultural expectations. This was illustrated to me by a discussion we had one Arabic class, when our teacher, as part of our education, wanted to take us to a Lebanese restaurant. She and some others felt it was acceptable for us all, male and female, to go together; however, others said that the men would have to sit at one table and women at another because men and women should not be socialising, and several women said they would prefer to have an all-women party so that they could relax and take off their hijab. Each was speaking from their own personal faith perspective and choosing to live out their interpretation of Islam. Sadly, with this and the difficulty several mothers had, including myself, of evening childcare provision, the meal never happened. Not all my encounters with Muslims have involved segregation however; I have been able to share meals, debates, lectures and other experiences with Muslim men present, and have been able to talk one-to-one with Muslim men about their faith and practice. I have found that in doing so I have wanted to respect the Qur'anic instruction on both sexes to practise modesty, and over the years have noticed myself more and more influenced by this, particularly in the way I dress.

Originally, I believed the hijab and *niqab*, covering the face also, and other forms of veiling to be instruments of oppression, or the reduction of the female into an object of desire that must be covered. Sometimes I still think veiling is, but of the women I have discussed this with, some choose not to wear the hijab and others have chosen to put on the hijab as a statement of faith, and it is they who are the ardent believers, their husbands taking the lead from their wives. This was the case with the women in the Arabic class. Since my visit to the Shi'a mosque I have on occasion taken to wearing hijab in public myself. I began this practice in response to the 7/7 bomb factory incident, which impacted so strongly on the community around All Hallows Church. Ray describes the fear and persecution to which Muslims were subjected following this news, and the community response to demonstrate unity, which led to the two peace marches. I took part in both of these, and took the photos that were later used for publicity, including plenty of Ray striding around with a megaphone! On the second march on the Saturday, I met an elderly Muslim woman who had stopped because some chewing gum was stuck to the sole of her shoe; I took the shoe and cleaned it for her, gave it back in exchange for a big hug and we walked together as she talked about her life, her children – a daughter turned out to be one of the women involved in organising the march – and the area of Hyde Park. The whole river of people flowing through the streets were relating in much the same way, spontaneous friendships forming because we wanted them to; old friendships aired for all to see: the world had to be shown that we were not split by the scaremongering, but united.

On the following Monday, I found myself reflecting on the powerful sense of solidarity that grew from the gathering, and how much confidence it generated. I wondered how it would feel to do the opposite, and walk not proudly as part of a great, banner-waving procession, but alone in a quiet, individual expression of solidarity. I found myself putting on my hijab very deliberately and as neatly as I could, to step out into the city and prayer-walk the streets alone. As I walked, I felt moved to words of penance, and prayed the Jesus Prayer: 'Lord Jesus Christ, have mercy on me a sinner.' It occurred to me, and still challenges me now, that this is a Christian calling to side with the marginalised, the victimised and the oppressed. It is something a Christian woman can choose to do, not out of the uncomfortable sense of subordination we have wrestled with as a consequence of certain passages in the Epistles, but as an act of willingness to step into the experience, the world, of the other in some small way. I have found this a humbling act, and a confusing one too: I have to be clear in my own mind why I am wearing the hijab, so that I can talk to those who ask.

Something Ray shares deeply about is his experience of Ramadan. Again, this is a point where our experiences both meet and differ. I had fasted during the day I visited the Shi'a mosque for the first time, and the following year – the year Ray kept a journal of Ramadan – I also fasted, inspired by the content of some of Ray's sermons and discussions at the time. Ray describes a deepening of relationship with Muslim friends who welcomed him, and encouraged him to step into the privacy of their mosques and homes to share food and their faith, and I think it is a testimony to Ray's sincerity and loving humility that he was – and is – able to be drawn in by members of another faith to come so close to being able to experience faith as they do, without in any way compromising his own, but rather, deepening it. I felt very inspired by this willingness to enter into the experience of 'the other', and by his determination, but found myself far more on the periphery. I didn't live in a Muslim area, and the friends I had made, rather than being available to talk and meet up, were busier than usual, and almost entirely wrapped up in family matters, particularly the preparation of the all-important evening fast-breaking meal. Ramadan wasn't a time for them to discuss what it meant to them but a time to get on with it. So to me, it became a time to notice from the outside the importance of shared community experience, a bonding, strengthening act of self-discipline. I actually found Ramadan a struggle much of the time. Fasting made me feel tired, so much so that by the end of a day's work on an empty stomach I was afraid to drive home, as I felt so light-headed. There was also the frustrating challenge of trying to find a quiet place to pray during the day, at work. Had I been a Muslim, I could have requested a clean, quiet place to use, and I know it would have been respected. As it was, I found myself unable to relax into prayers when at work, and I knew that without prayer, the fasting was of limited value, which led to doubts over the worth of the whole day's exercise. In short, I realised how extremely difficult it must be to live as a Muslim in isolation, I realised how strong the desire to pray becomes, and how hard it is to go hungry day after day. There has to be a very good reason for it: friends have since described Ramadan as a joyful time of self-cleansing, a kind of MOT for the body. I took it as an act of willpower, that first year, and struggled my way through out of stubbornness because I wanted to know how it felt. I knew there must be spiritual benefits and I wanted to experience them. In a sense, the stubbornness paid off, because I did go deeper into my own spirituality; Ramadan did become a holy month for me where I really did make an effort to read the Qur'an, follow a regular prayer routine, discipline myself to fast and to simplify my consumption, and to have regard for my speech and thoughts. It led me to consider Paul's admonition to 'pray without ceasing', and later, to take up the Christian practice of saying a Daily Office: Morning and Evening Prayer is the pattern I have now settled into rather than the more monastic requirement of five or more times a day, but like Ray I appreciate how the Muslim discipline is for all members of the faith family not just clergy. I have since seen, through spending time with other women friends, how observance of the prayer routine becomes a need and a joy. I more recently had the privilege of being welcomed into the homes of Muslim women I had befriended whilst studying Arabic, and was struck by the way they supported one another so lovingly, to make sure all responsibilities were met: the baby was passed between them – and I got my turns at baby-holding too – so that each sister could take some quiet time away from the domesticity, to pray. Being part of that sisterhood was one of the elements of Islam that most attracted me: I would dearly have loved to belong to such a group of friends when my son was small, to feel so supported in keeping God at the centre of my day.

I feel that Ray is right in suggesting that Islam offers a challenge and a corrective to Christianity – our fasts, in comparison, are pretty feeble. In fact, as a vegan, according to traditional Christian definitions, I am fasting all the time, which seems a bit of a cop-out: penance, self-discipline, self-examination and subordination of physical desires to spiritual pursuits exist in the history of Christianity and are part of the real nitty-gritty of the faith. But what do we do? Lent becomes a time to give up chocolate, or take up jogging around the block, and Advent is a time to put up Christmas decorations and light candles. There is a pressing call to explore Christian fast periods in the light of Ramadan, to consider how deeply we could go into our faith if we committed as communities to supporting one another in prayer, in self-denial and, as Ray says, maybe not so much in Bible study, which is ongoing anyway, but in coming to Christ, meditating on what *islam*, surrender to Christ, to God, really means.

Whilst Ramadan was a time for Ray to get very deeply involved in Muslim life, my opportunities came more through the circle of friends I made through studying Arabic for a year and a half. My motivation for learning Arabic was mainly to be able to read and learn more about something I had discovered quite a long time earlier to be a real spiritual treasure: the Ninety-Nine Beautiful Names of Allah. (Although I did briefly entertain a rather more unrealistic ambition of being able to read the Qur'an in Arabic!) I had begun to meditate on the names using a translation of Al-Ghazali, and had found that doing so transported me at times to sublime moments of spiritual peace and inspiration: I knew through opening myself in prayer that they had an intrinsic value, and was drawn out of a mystical desire to get closer to God to learn them by heart. I had begun to learn the sounds of the names and their simplified meanings – Allah, Ar-Rahmaan, Ar-Raheem, Al-Malik, Al Qodoos, As-Salaam – but being able to read and write them in the proper Qur'anic Arabic mattered to me as part of honouring the holiness I recognised in them. I knew them, through prayer, to be a revelatory gift. Although I reached a point where I could not keep up with the Arabic lessons and stopped going, I did get to the point I wanted to, and it is a joy to me to be able to enter into this Islamic revelation at a mystical level, confident that it is of God. As a Christian, part of me wants to suggest that there is more to God than the ninety-nine names in the list – but that does not stop me in any way engaging with the list as it stands, because it enriches my prayer life and speaks to my soul. At the time of writing I have learned 55 of the 99, and some of my Muslim sisters have encouraged me kindly, by assuring me that one who learns them all is promised a place in Paradise: a beautiful promise for a Muslim to repeat to a Christian, and words which I treasure. Given that I do feel the names to be icon-like in the way they open windows for the soul to experience the Divine, Ray's writing challenges me to ask myself if I can go further and accept the source of the names itself – the Qur'an – also to be Divine revelation. Addressing this question has prompted me to study further, seeking an intellectual answer. But I think that my gut feeling has to take precedence, which is that in my personal experience the people of the Qur'an are a lovely and loving people, prayerful and God-centred, so much so that they present a challenge to me and I believe to the church, to look at our own capacity to hold God at the centre of our lives with such intensity, and therefore the scripture they treasure so passionately is most certainly holy.

I was not aware, until Ray drew my attention to it, of the inspiration St Francis seems to have gained from the ninety-nine names; neither was I aware of St Francis's peaceful visit to the Sultan the Crusaders were at war with, nor of his teaching to the friars regarding appropriate conduct for Christians among Muslims. This intrigued me so much that I undertook to find out more about St Francis, seeing his approach to encounter with Islam to be a truly radical tool for Christian development of humble, loving relationship, and entirely what is needed in this current climate of mistrust and misrepresentation of Islam and Muslims.

I feel indebted to Ray for writing a book not only that is moving and challenging, but that has ministered to my faith in many ways, urging me to go deeper into Christianity through daring to go deeper into Islam, and to do that not just by looking from the outside, but by trying to find ways in, through a genuine desire to respect and to listen, and to respond lovingly to the challenge that Islam and *islam* present.

Chapter nine

The closest in amity

Hussein Mehdi

In the beginning was Lebanon

Prior to the Lebanese civil war I lived in Jalala, a small town in the Bekaa Valley, lying almost halfway on the main route between Beirut and Damascus. My family moved to Lebanon from Iraq to set up a carpet manufacturing plant because the Iraqi government of the day had revoked an earlier granted licence to import the machinery from Belgium. The year we moved was 1969 and I was seven years old. A coup in Baghdad the previous year had brought the notorious Baath Party to power. I was too young to know or even care about what was going on in Iraq at the time.

I went to a school in the picturesque city of Zahle, famous for its many cafés, restaurants and ice-cream parlours carved out of the boulders of Wadil Arayesh, a 1-mile strip of ravine on the banks of the narrow, fast-flowing Bardoni River. We would spend many weekends in the summer holidays enjoying the small amusement park and the delicious Lebanese *mezza*: titbits of food such as houmous, dolma, fresh salad, tabouleh and baba ghanoog.

Our long school bus would struggle through the narrow winding roads to reach the hilltop school. From there one could see the olive groves and vineyards as well as the red rooftops of this bustling but tranquil city. Zahle was a mainly Christian city and the private school I attended was run by an American evangelical mission. The 1000 or more pupils attending the school came from far-reaching towns and villages and from all religious backgrounds, Christian Maronite, Eastern Orthodox and Armenian, Sunni and Shi'a Muslims. Looking at the location recently with Google Earth brought back many conflicting memories of my early years.

It was a happy mixed community, until the many political factions striving for power under catchy but dividing slogans and the intricate politics of the Palestinian problem brought tension to the peaceful communities living in the small towns of the Bekaa Valley. One would hear of flying roadblocks here and there where gunmen of opposing political factions would stop cars and kidnap men of Christian or Muslim denomination, the fate of whom would be in the hands of aggressive young men. Hundreds would die needlessly through tit-for-tat exercises.

During the civil war, Abu Jihad, a prominent Palestinian military aide to the late Yasser Arafat, who was later assassinated in Tunisia by the Mossad, had taken over an empty apartment on the top floor of our building. His family would stay there on odd occasions as it was used as one of his many hideouts. I remember once sneaking a scary glimpse of Arafat surrounded by a few armed bodyguards from my bedroom window, just after sunrise as he was leaving the building after a short unannounced visit to Abu Jihad. My father and the other families living in the building were worried for the residents' safety, fearing that the Israeli air force would bomb the building. We would on occasion find ourselves hurrying for safety to Damascus at short notice at the first sign of looming danger.

Two of our neighbours in Jalala were a middle-aged Christian couple, who lived in a small flat in a 3-storey building owned by a relatively well-off Christian-Armenian immigrant family. The husband, a taxi driver, had moved to our area from the predominantly Christian town of Jezzin in south Lebanon soon after the start of the civil war in 1975, with his wife and two young children, a boy and his 8-year-old sister, Marie. Her name is still stuck in my memory as very often during the long summer holidays, I would hear Marie's mum shout loudly for her daughter: *'Ya Marie, waynik, ya Marie?'* ('Oh Marie, where are you, oh Marie?') Marie would sometimes play outside with other children from the mixed Muslim-Christian community, or she would be in our house sampling some of the unfamiliar Iraqi dishes – and then rush back home to her mum with a plateful of *kubba* (a cone-shaped crust of mashed rice stuffed with meat, raisins and almonds and shallow-fried to a crisp yellow-orange colour) that my mum had prepared for us. Marie's mum would then return the plate full of some of the speciality food she had made for lunch.

One fateful afternoon word spread in the neighbourhood that Marie's dad was stopped at a roadblock as he was returning home from a job; his fate was uncertain. There was pandemonium and panic in the air. Neighbours gathered to offer support to Marie's mum. An hour later, Marie's home was filled with screams and wailing. Her dad was confirmed dead and his body was brought to the house in a coffin. The young peaceful family had to pack their belongings in a rush and leave for their town, with the body escorted by a few neighbours. Marie's shattered family only returned one more time, a few weeks after the murder of her father, to remove the rest of their furniture. We never heard from them again.

A sense of déjà vu

The memories of the civil war in Lebanon suddenly came to life again in my mind some 28 years later, when in February 2004 my cousin Muwafaq would frequently drive Ray and me through the narrow streets of the Adhamiya district of Baghdad at night, as we travelled from his house to my granddad's old home in Kadhimiya, lying on the opposite bank of the Tigris River. The walls of some of the houses in Adhamiya carried ominous messages: 'Long Live The Hero Of Islam – Saddam', 'We Die But Saddam Lives'. I berated Muwafaq for his decision to drive us through these creepy and unsafe streets: 'What if a flying roadblock springs up and someone recognises we have an English priest with us?' Muwafaq, although having lived through many wars in Iraq as well as lengthy sanctions, had not really experienced a civil war before and did not appreciate what could happen at a moment's notice. The fate of Marie's dad and the many kidnapped Lebanese was strikingly vivid in my mind then. Muwafaq would tell us not to worry. On one occasion, in order to provide us with a sense of security, he pulled out an old Kalashnikov and placed it next to his seat. Ray politely and calmly told him that he couldn't travel with a weapon, as Jesus would not be happy with this. A short exchange of words ensued and Muwafaq acceded, only to clandestinely place the gun in the boot of the car. He obviously felt that Ray's passive approach would not cut any ice with the dangerous gunmen of Baghdad. I didn't feel that a gun in the boot of the car would have helped us in any confrontation. It would be better to resort to a prayer at that point.

Karbala: how can we forget?

On several occasions during our two-week stay in Iraq we faced potential dangers that could have erupted with fateful consequences. The closest we came to death was when a massive suicide attack took place in Karbala on Ashura day. Ray and I, along with some of my relatives, were only half a mile away from the place where the bombers struck just before midday. As we paced closer to the scene we witnessed open-top vans speeding out of the city, rushing the injured to hospital. I tried to calm a young woman who was shaken and crying: 'Don't worry,' I said, 'the bombs went off far away in the fields. No one is hurt.' That was what we had heard en route, but she sobbed back: 'What are you saying? I saw people cut and dying.'

The senseless, hate-filled attack killed and maimed at least 350 innocent men, women and children commemorating the day when the massacre of their 3rd Holy leader (Imam) and 72 of his family and followers took place in 680 AD. Imam Hussein, the second son of Ali and Fatima, the sole daughter of the Prophet Muhammad from his marriage with Khadija, was killed in Karbala at the hands of a several thousand-strong army gathered by the Muslim Caliphate-ruling establishment.

This establishment showed complete disregard for the esteemed position of Imam Hussein in the hearts and minds of Muslims throughout the territories of the vast Muslim empire. The army surrounded Imam Hussein's caravan of men, women and children en route from Mekkah to Kufa in Iraq. They demanded his absolute allegiance to the new Caliph, Yazeed, grandson of the Meccan tribal leader most at odds with the Prophet Muhammad's call. Imam Hussein took a heroic historical stand, preferring death to giving political and spiritual legitimacy to the new corrupt establishment. He said: 'The likes of me does not give allegiance to the likes of him.' This massacre still reverberates in the Muslim conscience after thirteen centuries, and has gorged out the hearts of those who do not wish for this memory to be commemorated by centuries of hate, manifesting itself as human bombs exploding on the streets of Baghdad and Karbala, walked by sympathisers of Imam Hussein and his family, on every Shi'a occasion since the fall of Saddam.

A film crew from Channel 4, who were producing a documentary on Ashura – 'Karbala, City of Martyrs' – were also with us in the city. I was one of the participants in the documentary and they were eager to get my reaction and that of others to the Ashura incident. They also needed to shoot a final scene with me and another person. This had to be rushed so they could quickly return to their safe house in the suburbs of Karbala. The ex-SAS bodyguard they hired to protect them would often stay in that house, as it was deemed safer for them to go out without him so as not to attract suspicion.

Ray was the only Christian priest in Karbala on Ashura day that year, the first Ashura day to be commemorated after the fall of Saddam. Over 3 million people had travelled (many on foot for days on end from the towns and villages of Iraq) to gather at the Shrine of Imam Hussein and that of his brother and standard-bearer Al-Abbass. The pilgrims would pay their respects and offer special visitation prayers. Ray's witness on that day and his insistence on mingling freely with the crowds, sometimes on his own, gave him the opportunity to get closer to the Shi'a Muslim psyche and understanding of Islam and the history of its development.

He even had the chance to debate with some people we met the merits of the extreme displays of passion that some Shi'a practise on Ashura day, such as self-flagellation and the shallow bloodletting from the top of the head. 'It is our way of displaying and communicating our extreme love and allegiance to Imam Hussein,' they eagerly explained to him. On our return to the UK, as we were waiting for our transfer flight at Amsterdam airport, Ray picked up the latest issue of *Time* magazine from the newsagent. He flicked through the pages and came towards me pointing to an image of a bloodletting scene in Karbala. 'Look at this,' he laughed. 'It is not actually as it is portrayed here, the image shows it as so violent, but it is not really like that at all,' he said.

And sympathy is what we need, my friend

I personally feel more comfortable listening to the softer colloquial rhyming poems that are sung to the crowds during the Ashura season, accompanied by a soft hand-beat to the chest. They capture the passion of the tragedy more subtly by transporting one to some of the poignant high points of Karbala mystery. Typical of these is the empathy poem which describes Imam Hussein's wife as she watches and mourns for her infant child, struck by an enemy arrow whilst in the arms of his father; the arrow was the only reply his enemies offered to repeated requests for water to quench the infant's thirst:

> 'Welaidy, welaidy ya Abdullah shnon sabih ibdemek.
> La liben yihsal la maay, bess dama't ummek.
> Sa'aou nishef maayil ayn, Abdullah yabni, Abdullah yabni.'

'My little child, my little child, oh Abdullah,
how you bathe in your blood.
I cannot offer you milk or water,
but only the teardrops of your sobbing mother.
Soon even my tears will run dry, oh my son Abdullah,
oh my son Abdullah.'

Equally moving is the poem about Imam Hussein's 13-year-old nephew Al-Qassim, who insisted on defending his uncle to the end:

'Yumma thukrini, min timur zaffat shabab.
M'nil eris mahroom, heniti dammil musaab
Shamaat shababi min yitafuha.
Heniti dammi, wil chefan daril turab
Yumma thukrini, min timur zaffat shabab.'

'O mother, remember me whenever you see a wedding march.
I have been deprived of my wedding, my henna[1] has become
the blood of this tragedy.
The candle of my youth is extinguished by the enemy;
my henna is my blood and my shroud will be the earth.
O mother, remember me whenever you see a wedding march.'

It is not just the naturally emotional who sing these melancholic poems, but also the hardy who gather around the reciter. In Karbala we witnessed this in the courtyard of Imam Hussein's mausoleum as the crowds collectively repeated the verses above. This flow of passion and sympathy cannot but soften the most solid of hearts as they participate in the service. Few can manage to hold their tears back from flowing down their cheeks. This annual culture of mourning moulds and shapes the psyche and attitude of a Shi'a Muslim and reinforces in them a sense of association with those who suffer or are victims of violence and oppression. They are brought up on this diet of passion from their early years, and on numerous occasions throughout the year.

On the other hand, why do some people target innocent civilians, whether they are sat on the London underground, on a bus, working in an office block in the Twin Towers or peacefully demonstrating their love for their spiritual leaders on the streets of Iraq, Pakistan or Afghanistan? How can they justify these murderous acts in order to promote or impose their political or religious interpretations, whilst at the same time link these acts to their religion? This question often crops up in my mind and it deserves an answer and some analysis. Maybe it is sheer ignorance and blatant disregard for the lives of others who differ from them, or a blind allegiance to a historical doctrine propagated by false heroes. Maybe it is based on messages of hate learnt in certain environments, justified by acts of violence from the other side. These acts may simply be purposefully orchestrated to terrorise ordinary people, instigate chaos and instability, in order to gain political advantage at the negotiating tables with the powers that be. If so, how can such tactics be justified?

I don't think there is a simple answer to this question, but whatever the answers, their legitimacy must be deeply rooted in the historical heritage and baggage that has been propagated for centuries.

There is a vivid contrast between the mindset of those who choose to associate themselves openly with victims and willingly accept the consequences of their allegiance to the family of the Prophet, and the mindset of those who choose to be with the victimisers or to watch from the sidelines.

The Shi'a tradition was kept alive not because of any temporal power they possessed (which was hardly significant when it occurred on rare and short-lived occasions), nor was it due to a financial power base that sustained them. The only reasonable explanation why the tradition still lives on, despite the extreme pressure put on Shi'as by the ruling establishments through the centuries, is because of the rich literary heritage they inherited from the Prophet's family and their sympathetic allegiance to Karbala.

Muhammad conquers Constantinople

I was in Turkey a few years ago and visited the Hagia Sophia Museum in Istanbul. The museum was originally the principal basilica of the Byzantine Empire. The empire was overrun by invading Muslim armies throughout the centuries, and was finally conquered by the army of Sultan Mehmet II in 1453 AD. The Eastern Orthodox church was then converted into a mosque, and remained so until the secular Turkish republic, established by General Kamal Ataturk at the end of the First World War after the collapse of the Ottoman Caliphate, turned it into a museum. I noticed many plaques in the grounds of the museum and inside the beautiful vast cathedral. These plaques had English and German translations. Only one plaque stood out. It was written in Arabic and translated only into Turkish – lest it offend the euro-spending tourists. The plaque read: *The Prophet Mohammad (blessings be on him) said: 'You shall conquer Constantinople; blessed is the army that conquers it and blessed is the commander of that army.'*

This narration (*hadith*) is included in some of the Muslim books of 'authentic' *hadith* and is relied upon as a saying of the

Prophet Muhammad. The narration appears in some of the books of tradition of the 'schools of thought' endorsed and legitimised by the Caliphate-ruling establishment. Imagine a ruling establishment, wanting to expand its imperial territory and keep its subjects engaged with an external enemy, creating a rallying point behind this leadership and a useful distraction from critical engagement in the internal affairs of the state. The advantages are immense: greater territorial acquisitions mean more tax revenues for the Caliph's coffers, and greater stability of the Caliphate means it can be handed down to future generations of the ruling family.

Shi'as and some Sunni researchers do not accept this *hadith* as the authentic words of Muhammad. It was probably fabricated after the coup that propelled the earlier adversaries of the Prophet into the power seat of the Muslim empire. For centuries Muslims have been engaged in military conquests in the name of spreading Islam. This violence has caused so much death and destruction that it cannot be ignored. Many Muslims are wrongly proud of this history and show a sense of extreme loss at the decline of this vast empire. Some groups today pursue violent means similar in their potency to those exercised by their grandfathers to bring back the glory of this hollow empire. They see Islam and Muslim history as being one and the same thing. They loathe anyone being critical of this history and calling into question the reputations of men regarded as established heroes in their minds. They ignore and brush over the incidents that clearly contradict the message of Islam and try to justify the actions of these heroes by any means possible. Some dare go so far as to claim that the sword of the Muslim Caliphate that killed Imam Hussein (so beloved and cared for by his grandfather Muhammad) was the 'sword of his grandfather', and that Yazeed was a legitimate successor of the Prophet, regardless of how he came to power: and as such anyone going against his rule deserves to be dealt with by the Caliphate in the manner it chooses.

Muslims are very resentful of the idea promoted in certain Christian circles that Islam is a religion spread by the sword. They flatly reject this and would spin the historical events in such a way so as to bring a shiny gloss to them. They would claim either that conflict was the order of the day and Muslims were only trying to defend their weak, newly established base from powerful empires surrounding them to the east and west, or that the Muslim armies only gave the opportunity for people ruled by tyrannical rulers to be free, and that those people were eager to come into the new faith of Islam as liberated peoples. I cannot understand how, at the same time, Iraqis are chastised for accepting the freedom offered by the invading armies of the Coalition forces from the hands of a tyrant such as Saddam – whom many Arabs and Muslims still regard as a hero equal to those idolised heroes of Muslim history. It appears that as long as the tyrant is a Muslim then his tyranny must be tolerated. If you think I am being facetious, then I invite you to research the criteria for eligibility to be a caliph in Muslim scholarly literature. Many scholars advocate the sword as a legitimate means of acquiring power: and anyone reaching the mantle of leadership through this means must be obeyed by the ordinary masses.

However, I cannot see how judgement on the Muslim empire's spread can be levied by those whose territorial base was spread through the same means. The Muslim and Christian empires, like any other empire, were spread by violence – whether by the sword or the canon. How else can it be explained that huge territories were acquired in relatively short periods of time? The Muslims didn't exactly go to these nations with flowers, gifts and hugs and kisses. Nor did the Christians take gold nuggets and bullion to the indigenous populations of Central America. Yes, both civilisations can indeed claim worthy examples where non-violent methods were exercised to bring people into their respective faiths, whether in the far eastern territories visited by Muslim traders or in various territories around the globe visited by certain Christian missionaries.

Both civilisations can also point to examples of tragic oppression which have shaken human consciousness and have been catalysts for the spread of faith into the hearts of many. I believe this is what Ray found in the tragedy of Karbala. He could not but empathise with it as his heart was softened by the example of Jesus and it was broken in the presence of Lady Zaynab, the sister of Imam Hussein, when we visited her shrine in Zaynabiya near Damascus.

Zaynab breaks a heart open

We arrived late on a cold night at Damascus airport on our way to Iraq. Through my relatives, we had arranged for a car to pick us up from the airport and drive us down to Baghdad the same night, as it was safer to arrive in Iraq in the early morning. In early 1994 the main route from Syria to Iraq would from time to time be obstructed by bandits looking for cash or jewellery, rather than for men to kidnap and execute. The driver told us that the Syrian border with Iraq was closed and that we were unlikely to get through. He advised us to wait a couple of days until the situation was made clearer. He drove us to Zaynabiya, a small village some 10 kilometres outside Damascus, which had grown up around the burial place of Lady Zaynab – the heroine of Karbala and the protector of the women, children and youths who remained alive after the massacre. Lady Zaynab's caravan was captured by the Governor of Kufa, before being dispatched to Yazeed's capital, Damascus.

The eloquent speeches of Lady Zaynab, or those of the daughters of Imam Hussein, to the fiercely proud, arrogant Governor of Kufa or to the Caliph Yazeed, sat on his imperial throne in Damascus, reveal truly remarkable female characters, and are well worth reading for an appreciation of the contrast between the House of Hashim, from which the Prophet and his family descend, and their rivals, the House of Ummaya, from which Yazeed and the caliphs after him descended. Muslims' contradictory interpretations and viewpoints are rooted in this divide and in the power struggle that ensued after their Prophet died.

History is often written by the victors and it is they who define the outlook and views of ordinary folk and shape the future course of a nation. They do this through their established regime of oppression, their power institutions, their propaganda machine and their spending-power to buy allegiance. Muslim history is no different to any other history in this respect, except where the victims of oppression leave a lasting legacy that would constantly bear on the claims and plans of the victors. The tragedy of Imam Hussein and his family is one such powerful legacy that bears its fruit throughout the millennia and manifests itself in small but significant events, such as the ones witnessed by Ray and his church.

After having a quick sandwich in the only open café on the main road of Zaynabiya, Ray and I persuaded the driver to take us to the Iraqi border and risk the consequences. Within four hours we were at the border. The Syrian officer there said the border was closed to non-Iraqis and Ray could not be let in. He needed special permission from the Syrian Interior Ministry in Damascus. We had to go back to Damascus and wait. We stayed in one of the many hotel apartments in Zaynabiya. I said to Ray that Lady Zaynab was not happy with us for passing through her place without offering her a visit: she wanted us to visit her, that's why we couldn't get into Iraq the first time. He suggested that we go and visit the shrine. He bought a Syrian Koufiya male scarf to cover his long hair, as he was getting rather uneasy with the gazes of onlookers who hadn't come across a similar hairstyle before.

We entered the courtyard of the shrine but Ray was not sure whether it was OK for him to enter the main shrine. I wasn't sure either how the visiting pilgrims or the custodians of the shrine would react. I said to Ray to follow me and we entered the shrine after offering greetings and salams to Lady Zaynab. I went to offer a short prayer whilst Ray stood close to the main door, admiring the small mirror pieces laid in geometric patterns on the pillars and walls. The big dome, inscribed with verses from the Quran in delicate and artistic Arabic calligraphy, was raised high above the tomb, which was enclosed with large ornamental silver railings and topped with a gold cap donated by wealthy Shi'a businesses in the Gulf. People would hold on to the silver railings and offer prayers and promises to God. They believe that offering such prayers and promises in the presence of a saint as holy as Lady Zaynab hastens the solving of their dilemma, as God will look more favourably upon those who love and associate themselves with God-serving souls whom He loves and admires.

A small group of Iranian pilgrims had opened a circle near the tomb and started a song of lamentation for Lady Zaynab. I love the passionate and moving melancholic voices of Iranian singers. They reach the depths of my soul. I hadn't realised that it had also mesmerised Ray until I noticed him uncontrollably weeping as he looked at them. I didn't want to disturb him at the time, but after we left I asked him what had overcome him. He explains this clearly and eloquently in this book.

After exhausting the options of getting a permit from the Syrians, we decided to head to Iraq through Jordan. 'Welcome to Iraq' was the greeting of the passport officer on the Iraqi border, clearly looking for a cash handout as he gave us back our passports stamped for entry. We breathed a sigh of relief, but were still perturbed by the potentially dangerous route to Baghdad.

We faced the same problem with the Syrians on leaving Iraq. But this little setback gave us an opportunity to witness a very powerful reminder in Damascus of the deep historical influence shaping the developments in the newly emerging Iraq: the role of the suicide bomber.

Al-Hamidiya suicide bomber

We went to seek gifts for family from the most famous *souk* in Damascus. Souk Al-Hamidiya is an old *souk* running for about a mile. It ends in the Ummayad Mosque, a converted Christian church, which was the seat of power of Yazeed's Caliphate. This is where the caravan of Zaynab ended up, with the 73 heads of the men massacred in Karbala. They were carried on spears into the palace in a ceremonial fashion amongst jubilant crowds who believed them to be traitors to the Caliph; and as such, their women and children were slaves of war, and so brought in shackles to be sold in the slave market. Incidentally, in the middle of this mosque is a shrine to John the Baptist, whose head was also brought in a similar ceremonial manner.

We were welcomed into the shop of one shopkeeper, and he showed us intricately carved souvenirs made by experienced craftsmen. The shopkeeper was interested to find out where we came from. 'Iraq,' I said to him, 'and Ray is from England.' He was even more welcoming. 'I am from the Shahbandar family, the same family as Saddam's wife,' he boasted eagerly. 'Aha,' I replied, 'only if you know the story behind Saddam's marriage to this wife.' It is well known in Iraq that Saddam took a fancy to the wife of the head of Iraqi Airways, and that he forced him to divorce his wife so he could have her as his second wife. He had a son by her whom he named Ali.

The shopkeeper soon realised that I wasn't in favour of Saddam, but he remained friendly and continued his conversation. Very soon he took a wallet out of his back pocket and slipped out a picture of a young man with an uncut, long black beard. 'This is my brother,' he said, 'he died in Iraq.' 'How did he die?' we asked. 'He drove an ambulance full of explosives into the Red Cross building in Baghdad,' the shopkeeper replied. 'That's what we have been told by the resistance,' he continued. 'He didn't go on his own. It is all well organised and they are chosen for these missions. They had news that the Red Cross building was used by the Americans. My brother left a wife and two children behind and I am looking after them now.'

The Red Cross building was struck during Ramadan of 2003, a few months after the invasion of Iraq. The bombing made headline news and killed and injured nearly 70 people, if my memory serves me right.

By now I was even less impressed with this guy and his brother. 'You know something,' I said to him. 'It is such a shame that here we have a Christian from a foreign country with us who is not keen to spend a few dollars to buy his family a gift, but would rather give it to a charitable project in Iraq, yet the Arabs and the likes of your brother only gift us bombs that kill innocent people.' The shopkeeper was visibly shaken. He conceded that there was a lot of confusion in his head about whether his brother did the right thing. Whether he was a martyr in heaven or not. He said that when they were young they were fed in their mosques on a diet of hate for the Shi'as and told that they are not true Muslims. But now that he had grown older he had started thinking about things differently.

The next day I bought a relevant book from a shop in Zaynabiya and went back to the shopkeeper and gave it to him. 'Perhaps, if you read this, it will give more insight into who the Shi'as are,' I said, and walked out of his shop as he thanked us for the second visit and the gift.

Conclusion

I often reflect on my journey to Iraq with Ray. Both of us have used it to build bridges between the differing communities. It was the first time in my life that I spent three weeks with a Christian priest, eating, sleeping, visiting and talking to each other. At certain moments there was some tension in the air between us, especially on the Iraqi border or when travelling in the car in dangerous areas of Iraq. That was probably due to my anxiety and impatience. However, I feel that the experience has enriched my life and understanding of Christians. I sometimes engage in deep conversations with Ray, and I begin to wonder if the differences between us are mainly semantic and deep down we are very close to each other in our understanding of God. The following verse from the Quran often comes to mind:

> *And you shall find those closest to the believers in amity are those who say: "We are Christians"; that is because there are priests amongst them and virtuous monks, and they are free from arrogance.*
>
> *And when they hear the revelations, sent to the Messenger, you see their eyes flooded with tears as they recognise the truth therein; they pray: "Our Lord, do write us amongst them who bear witness."*

Chapter 5, verses 82–83

Footnote

1. Henna is a plant that produces a burgundy dye. In Eastern culture the dye is used to decorate the bride and groom's hands and feet on their wedding day.

Chapter ten

Lovers of Truth

Firdaws Khan

Having been involved in the anti-war movement in Leeds since 2001, I had come across Ray Gaston's name and that of All Hallows Church on a number of occasions, as the church became the strongest Christian voice in the city, making a clear stand against the war and campaigning for peace. With the ongoing 'War on Terror', this was a welcomed voice at the time and in times to come. The War of Terror, which provided and continues to provide the backdrop to our lives since 9/11, with a combination of violence, injustice, agony, anger, fear, confusion and, sadly, apathy surrounding the mass murder, the illegal and inhumane wars, waged in the guise of corrective military measures – to punish rogue states and to realign them and their butchered peoples to 'civilised' standards of 'democracy'.

And so it was through the anti-war grapevine that I became familiar with Ray Gaston; and whilst working on Ramadan Radio, I heard about his trip to Iraq in 2004. It was something about this man's essence that trickled through this grapevine; particularly the depth of his compassion and conviction moved me, and his consistency impressed me. He was not just another local community leader rolling out gestural sound-bites in times of high drama – he was clearly a man of action. I remember thinking that it would be useful to meet him and perhaps 'join forces' with such an individual and his church, as having been involved in interfaith and multi-faith circles for many years, I was acutely aware that a united-faith voice was

189

somewhat lacking in wake of the global violence and in the proliferation of the War of Terror.

I did not actually meet Ray Gaston until Ramadan in the autumn of 2006, when I organised a community *iftar* with my local Stop the War group in Harehills, which was titled 'A Reflection on Peace and Justice in Ramadan'.

The aim of the *iftar* was to bring people of different faiths and no faith together, to share in the spirit of Ramadan, which to me re-establishes a deep sense of peace[1], equality and justice in the hearts of those who seek the benefits of the practice. I sometimes call Ramadan the 'great equaliser', as somehow it feels that with an empty stomach we are all quickly brought to the same place, the same level and all become equal before our Creator. It does not matter if you are a prince or a pauper: you enter a discipline of giving up food and drink and allow yourself to be humble and vulnerable before your Lord and in relation to all others around you – so experiencing a sense of universal equality and justice.

I had invited Ray Gaston and Annie Heppenstall to share their experiences of fasting in Ramadan and I was moved by the accounts they shared. It was clear that they had not fasted simply as brotherly and sisterly gestures of fasting in solidarity with their Muslim neighbours. No, it was not fasting as outsiders to the tradition – but they had entered wholly into the spirit of fasting, seeking the depth of spiritual insight that can only come from being on the *inside*. It seemed that they had intended to ascertain the effects of the Ramadan tradition of fasting on their own spiritual barometers. Hence, in the Ramadan diary there are some very refreshing insights into rejuvenating and relinking to the old tradition of fasting in Christianity. I feel that the insights offer freshness and pick up a fineness of the experience that many of us Muslims ourselves do not always hold awareness of, since the seasoned practice of fasting in Ramadan can sometimes be absorbed into the background tapestry of our lives that we sometimes take for granted.

I found it interesting that the author comments on the Ramadan experience as being very much a 'communal' tradition of fasting. Although this is largely true, it is also important to say that since all forms of Islamic worship have at their core the direct relationship of the worshipper and Allah – it is also foremost a deeply individual experience and so rather like the example of Jesus (peace be upon him) fasting in the wilderness. Ramadan is the opportunity for us to traverse the *inner wilderness* of our own personal spiritual landscapes. This is highlighted by the practice of *Itiqaaf*, which involves retreating into silent reflection, prayer and contemplation in the last ten days of the month.

Rumi[2] relates to the practice of fasting, its healing benefits and to the process of taming our inner wilderness, as an attempt to polish and nurture the spirit:

Fast from thoughts, fast:
thoughts are the lion and the wild ass;
men's hearts are the thickets they haunt.
Fasting is the first principle of health;
restraint is superior to medication;
scratching only aggravates the itch.
Fast, and behold the strength of the spirit.
(Mathnawi I, 2909-11)

From the time of the communal *iftar*, the author and I became friends and I had the privilege of being invited to co-facilitate some workshops for the Peace School[3] in 2007 and in

2008, on Peace in Islam, and also some comparative text (the Quran and Bible) and dialogue workshops. We set about with the intention of sharing ideas and the interfaces of what our faiths informed us about peace, in an attempt to tap into some of the core understandings and essences of these concepts.

In the workshop on 'Islam and Peace', one of the exercises I had set upon was to derive some of the core essences of the concept of Peace by reflecting on some of the root words in Arabic relating to the word Peace (*Salam*). The origin is *As-Salam* (one of the ninety-nine names of Allah), and its stem is from the verb *Salima*, which means *to be whole, integral, complete, safe*. Hence, therein is a corollary of wholeness to the essence of Peace and the idea that *peacefulness* comes from our connection to *wholeness*, or when we are ourselves in harmony with, or *at one with, the whole*. This can be being at one with ourselves and our environment. But ultimately we are all individual integers of the greater *wholeness*, which exists as the integrity of the entire cosmos, behind which there is the Holiness (*Al-Quddus*), the Unity, which Muslims refer to as Allah.

From the above we followed another trajectory of Peace and pondered on the word *Shaheed*, which again originates from another of the ninety-nine names of Allah, *Ash-Shaheed, The Witness*. The word witness means someone who is present, so being witness to, means *to be present*. Again in relation to Peace – and in upholding the integrity of the universe and the world in which we exist – it becomes necessary for us, as citizens of the world, to be witnesses, *to be present*, to that wholeness (and Holiness) and totality of which we are all a part, and the Truth[4] which is held therein.

How ironic it is then to find that in the entirety of our lives we are mostly *not present* to the present moment and so mostly not at peace with ourselves or some other entity around us. Most of the time, we are not fully in awareness nor hold consciousness and so cannot be present to Truth nor to the Holiness.

Our perception of what happens in the moment is frequently aberrated by the past or our concern for something in the future. Our lens through which we view and experience the world is mostly not free from our distorted egos and our preoccupying delusions. We are jammed up with our preconceived ideas, judgements, hang-ups and prejudice, some of which may be not just our personal ones – but also those effects we inherit from the collective – our environment, culture and even the hearsay of our religions. By the latter, I mean the kind of dominant myths that exist about and within religion[5], which sometimes have sat around and existed for so long that they continue to misinform us, as they ferment in our psyches and indeed are passed on from psyche to psyche.

These are not only things that we think are true about our own religions, but also the beliefs that invalidate other religions and so affect the way we see 'the other' and the way of the other. Moreover, we intellectually conform and civilise our thinking to align ourselves to the common default position. We allow ourselves to hold a benign resignation to popular political correctness which lulls us out of consciousness and into a semi-detached numbness, and so we become semi-detached in our connection to humanity and the whole around us.

It is this numbness that seems to have become a requisite for being in today's world – a survival code of keeping your head down, so long as you are doing okay, as it is best not to awaken a consciousness that may make it hard to grapple with the injustices of the day.

When we multiply the effects of all these influences we can see why we are pacified into a security blanket of collective conscience – only it is a false sense of security, as it stops us from using our own reason-gifted minds, seeking with the entirety of our hearts and with the whole of our beingness the Truth – a Truth and consciousness that could revitalise our faith and transform our fear and anxiety into hope and a deeper confidence in our humanity. How different the world could be if only we had the courage to uphold the integrity of the world in which we exist.

It is this semi-detached numbness, and indeed a kind of semi-detached madness, which has prevailed within the dominant political culture throughout this period since 9/11; which reminds me of a quote by Edmund Burke:

> *All that is necessary for evil to succeed is that good men do nothing.*

This statement has haunted me deeply throughout this period of the War of Terror, as it tells a deeply disturbing truth of how such a war has been allowed to proliferate. Indeed it has been allowed to escalate as there are far too many of us 'good men'[6] who have allowed the slumber of semi-detachedness to numb us out of consciousness and into the smouldering evil of silence in the wake of mass injustice. Indeed, this is the evil which we commit against our own souls and against the whole – of which we are a part – as we fail to be fully present and be witnesses to uphold Truth.

The antidote to this evil is commitment to Truth, the responsibility of being part of the whole and the courage for each of us to be a witness, for it is by being witnesses to Truth that will allow Peace to prevail.

Throughout the book the underlying current which the author communicates is the struggle (jihad) to be a witness. This is what makes the book such an important one for the time we live in, for it not only attempts to challenge and deconstruct some of the prevailing belief systems but also highlights the powerfulness of being a witness and exemplifies the potential of witnessing as a healing antidote to all that wounds us and casts us into the darkness of worldly despair. It is this positive effect of being a witness which is summed up in the Quranic verse:

> *And those who believe In Allah and His messengers –*
> *They are the Sincere (Lovers of Truth) and*
> *Witnesses who testify*
> *In the eyes of their Lord:*
> *They shall have their Reward*
> *And their Light.*
> *But those who reject Allah*
> *And deny Our signs –*
> *They are the Companions of Hell-fire. (57:19)*

In fact, I find there is a great deal in the book which is in tandem with the spirit of Quranic counselling, such as the resistance to passive compliance to ancestral forms of religion (as already referred to above) and resistance to mere compulsion in faith:

> *Let there be no compulsion*
> *In religion: Truth stands out clear from error:*
> *Whoever rejects Evil and believes in Allah*
> *Has grasped the most trustworthy Handhold that never breaks.*
> *And Allah hears and knows all things. (2:256)*

I would therefore say that the kind of faith that is being sought after in the above verse is indeed the kind of radical faith that the author consistently refers to and seeks to promote in the book. It is a form of faith which is fully alive in the witness, with an open and compassionate heart, a faith which can vitalise and restore us from our dis-eased detachment and all the dogma which rules the world and seeks to divide and devour the sanctity of humanity.

The book is also a testimony to what we can achieve when we allow our hearts[7] to be the prisms of our minds. And so it is the medley of beauty and the power of love and heartfulness which the book conveys so strongly. Although written for and primarily aimed at a Christian audience, as a Muslim I am touched, moved and inspired by the spirit of the book, by the insights of a traveller who clearly seeks to voyage into the heart of Islam, not just as an intellectual exercise but as a living experience. I would therefore recommend that the book be read by Muslims, as it is a beautifully written spiritual adventure that will resonate with all those who are seekers of a spiritual path, and at the same time it is scholarly, courageous, honest and deeply earnest in asking the questions most will not ask and in sharing the journey of a heart seeking Peace.

Firdaws Khan,
September 2008

Footnotes

1. Fasting is a state that can promote peace through physical and emotional cleansing. It not only quells negative emotional states, internal violence and hyperactive egos; it feeds the soul and nurtures a mindfulness and awareness of the fragility of our natures as well as the power of giving something up out of love for something higher than ourselves. It is a code for communal peacefulness, in that fighting and making of war is forbidden during the holy month.

2. Jalaluddin Rumi – thirteenth-century Persian poet and Islamic scholar. Quotation from Rumi from *The Pocket Rumi*, Mevlana Jalaluddin Rumi, edited by Kabir Helminski, Shambhala Pocket Classics, 2001.

3. The Peace School is an initiative set up by Christians to encourage what they call 'Shalom Activism' www.peaceschool.org.uk

4. Truth in Arabic is *Haqq*; it originates from one of the ninety-nine names of Allah, *Al-Haqq* – The Truth. It is an attribute which is also complimentary to *Ash-Shaheed*. In order to apprehend Truth, we have to be present to it and so be active witnesses.

5. The Quran is unequivocal in advising against blindly following ancestral patterns of religion:

Whenever we sent a Warner before thee to any people,
The wealthy ones among them
Said: 'We found our fathers following a certain religion,
And we will certainly follow in their footsteps.' (43:23)

6. And, of course, good women.

7. Quranically, the heart, *qalb*, is the seat of knowing and the intelligent centre of our being and certainly the epicentre of our search for knowledge and Truth.

Appendix

Some resources for engaging with the Qur'an, written by Muslims or taking an approach that is sensitive to and knowledgeable about how Muslims engage with the Qur'anic revelation:

Good books on the Qur'an by Muslims

The Qur'an: A User's Guide, Farid Esack, One World, 2005

A very good all-round introduction from a Muslim committed to a faith-activist and liberationist perspective but who also undertook traditionalist Islamic studies. Esack was a leading Muslim activist in the anti-apartheid struggle in South Africa and has been involved in activism on war, imperialism and AIDS – an interfaith activist who has also studied Christian theology.

How to Read the Qur'an, Mona Siddiqui, Granta, 2007

Muslim academic's accessible introduction to the Qur'an. An interfaith practitioner who has featured in recent years as one of the main speakers at the Greenbelt Arts Festival.

'Believing Women' in Islam: Unreading Patriarchal Interpretations of the Qur'an, Asma Barlas, University of Texas Press, 2002

This is a more challenging read than the other two books but well worth the effort – a brilliant reading of the Qur'an from a woman's perspective emphasising the radically egalitarian and anti-patriarchal nature of its teachings. Asma Barlas is part of a leading group of women scholars challenging readings of Islam based on Western media stereotypes and cultural patriarchy.

Reading/hearing the Qur'an

Approaching the Qur'an: The Early Revelations, Michael Sells, White Cloud Press, 2007

This is an excellent starting place. The book goes through each of the surahs, the shorter Meccan surahs of early Qur'anic revelation, that a young Muslim would learn as they first became familiar with the Qur'an. Sells translates these surahs and has a scholarly but accessible commentary on each. The book also contains a CD with recitations of some of the surahs by world-renowned reciters.

The Book of Revelations: A Sourcebook of Themes from the Holy Qur'an, edited by Kabir Helminski, The Book Foundation, 2005

A good next step, with commentaries on a large number of selected passages by well known modern scholars.

The Qur'an, translated by M.A.S. Abdel Haleem, Oxford World Classics, 2008

A good modern, accessible translation of the whole Qur'an

The Message of the Qur'an, Book Foundation, 2008

The Arabic text with transliteration, translation and commentary by modern scholar Muhammad Asad – for deeper engagement.

Ray Gaston

Contributors

Annie Heppenstall is recently (2008) married, to Ray Gaston, and enjoys living with him and her son in an Islamically rich area of Birmingham where 'love your neighbour' comes alive through interfaith trust and friendship-building. She is the author of two books, *Wild Goose Chase* and *Reclaiming the Sealskin* (Wild Goose Publications).

Firdaws Khan was born in Kashmir in a Sunni Muslim family. She was exposed to a diversity of faith and culture, as well as to Sufism, at an early age, and so has carried an empathy for other faiths and an affinity for spiritual traditions in Islam. She lives in Leeds, where she has been a community activist and is involved in the anti-war movement locally. She enjoys taking inspiration from her work as a homeopath and as a freelance training consultant, from playing with children and from retreating to the mountains from time to time.

Hussein Mehdi was born in Baghdad, Iraq and moved to Lebanon at the age of seven. He spent his teenage years there and experienced the early years of the civil war. At the age of 15 he moved to England to continue his education. Hussein founded the Iraq Solidarity Fund with Ray Gaston, which raised money for small local projects inside Iraq between 2005 and 2007.

Salma Yaqoob is Vice Chair of Birmingham Stop the War Coalition and is the Leader of the Respect Party. In 2006 she was elected as a city councillor in Birmingham City Council. Salma Yaqoob is a regular commentator in the media on current affairs and has appeared on BBC TV's *Question Time* and BBC Radio's *Any Questions*. She is the author of 'Muslim Women and the War on Terror', *Feminist Review* (No. 88), 2008.

Lightning Source UK Ltd.
Milton Keynes UK
30 January 2010

149328UK00002B/2/P